Dear Author

letters of hope

Dear Author

letters of hope

edited by **joan f. kaywell**

with an introduction by
catherine ryan hyde

philomel books

the letters in this compilation have been edited
to protect the identity of their composers

PHILOMEL BOOKS
A division of Penguin Young Readers Group
Published by The Penguin Group
Penguin Group (USA) Inc., 375 Hudson Street, New York, NY 10014, U.S.A.
Penguin Group (Canada), 90 Eglinton Avenue East, Suite 700, Toronto, Ontario, Canada M4P 2Y3
(a division of Pearson Penguin Canada Inc.).
Penguin Books Ltd, 80 Strand, London WC2R 0RL, England.
Penguin Ireland, 25 St. Stephen's Green, Dublin 2, Ireland (a division of Penguin Books Ltd.)
Penguin Group (Australia), 250 Camberwell Road, Camberwell, Victoria 3124, Australia
(a division of Pearson Australia Group Pty Ltd).
Penguin Books India Pvt Ltd, 11 Community Centre, Panchsheel Park, New Delhi—110 017, India.
Penguin Group (NZ), Cnr Airborne and Rosedale Roads, Albany, Auckland 1310, New Zealand
(a division of Pearson New Zealand Ltd).
Penguin Books (South Africa) (Pty) Ltd, 24 Sturdee Avenue, Rosebank,
Johannesburg 2196, South Africa.
Penguin Books Ltd, Registered Offices: 80 Strand, London WC2R 0RL, England.

Library of Congress Cataloging-in-Publication Data
Dear author : letters of hope / edited by Joan F. Kaywell. p. cm.
1. Teenagers—Books and reading—United States. 2. Teenagers—Correspondence. 3. Authors,
American—20th century—Correspondence. 4. Young adult literature—Appreciation—United
States. 5. Authors and readers—United States. 6. Young adult fiction, American. I. Kaywell, Joan F.
Z1037.A1D28 2007   028.5'5—dc22   2006021050

ISBN 978-0-399-23705-8
10 9 8 7 6 5 4 3 2 1
First Impression

TABLE OF CONTENTS

To my son, Stephen Matthew Kaywell,
my hope and joy

To these authors, who dare to write
about tough issues in hopes of
helping those who read about them

To well-intentioned censors of these authors,
that they come to realize these books save lives
and are not the problem

And to Michael Green and Courtenay Lewis
for not giving up on me!

In Memory of Ted Hipple
1935–Thanksgiving Day 2004

ALAN and the Authors Wish You Well Eternally

INTRODUCTION

Now that I've written the book *Pay It Forward*, a novel about a twelve-year-old boy who changes the world through multiplying acts of kindness, things have changed in my life. Now that the book has become a movie, starring Kevin Spacey, Helen Hunt, and Haley Joel Osment, everything seems to be going my way. Now that the book and movie have spawned a nonprofit educational foundation and a real-life social movement, it's easy to be fooled into thinking that I know exactly who I am, and I always have.

If only my story were so simple. Here's the part you don't see.

I can still remember where I was, what I was thinking, and what I was feeling when I crossed over that invisible line. In one moment, I was transformed from a play-by-the-rules kid to someone more shadowy and difficult to define. I could have gone anywhere from there—that's the problem. But the obvious direction seemed to be down.

The setting was a classroom. I remember where I was sitting. I can visualize the blackboard to which I probably seemed to pay attention. I remember the teacher but not her name. She was in a bad mood. She abused and embarrassed me in front of my classmates, not because I had misbehaved, but because she was fed up with the whole class and looking to make an example of someone.

I was eleven years old.

The moment hit me like a wave, and washed me under, and turned me over a few times, and—like a person who has been tumbled in the deep water—I felt a palpable loss of direction. I knew if I headed for the surface, it might not be the surface at all. It might be the bottom. Nothing was written in stone anymore. There was nothing in which to invest faith. I felt in that instant that everything I had been taught was a lie. I wasn't going to play by the rules grown-ups had taught me, not anymore. Because they didn't work, I might just as well write my own.

I had become—though we didn't use the phrase way back then—an "at-risk youth."

Of course, this moment wasn't as sudden or isolated

as it seemed. Many years of alienation had added one straw after another to my back. This straw wasn't even the worst. It was, however, the last.

Home had always been a battleground. And, like most battlegrounds, each combatant was preoccupied with his or her own survival. I had a sense that I could disappear—figuratively, of course—and no one would notice. And, in a figurative sense, I did disappear, at quite an early age.

My peer group had long been brutal in their treatment of me. I seemed to invite them to abuse me in some way I couldn't recognize and untangle. I wore dark clothing and sat in the corner, hoping to become even more invisible. Attention had long ago taken on a distinctly negative connotation.

By the time I hit high school I found cigarettes, alcohol, drugs, and a circle of friends with attitudes to match my own.

Where I might have ended up without Mr. Horowitz, I can't say.

Lenny Horowitz was my sophomore English and creative writing teacher. He was only about ten years older than the class. He had a full beard. He got us reading novels and plays written in this century, peopled with characters far to the left of mainstream. He made us write. He let me call him Lenny. He stayed after school for half an hour or so, anytime I felt like talking.

One day Lenny read my essay out loud in front of the class. It was intended to be a humorous piece, which is always risky. Everybody laughed, including Lenny. He told the class my work was clever. Later I found out that he went back to the staff lounge and told all my other teachers I could write.

He told me I was good at something. And I respected him, so I believed him.

I'd love to tell you that my life turned cleanly around on that day. I'd love to say I charted a course and straightened myself out. But we all know life is not that easy. I had to invest two decades in fighting my way out of drug and alcohol abuse and other related troubles. I was nearly thirty-four by the time I got clean and sober. But for those twenty years I had something, something without which I might not have survived. I had a dream of something I thought I could be, planted by someone who believed in me.

It took me nearly two years to put my head back on straight and clean up the wreckage of my past. Even then, I might not have seized that dream, if not for Harvey.

Harvey was another recovering alcoholic. I was between jobs, looking to make a real change, embark on a new career. Harvey and I were discussing my possible employment options when he looked me in the eye and said, "You strike me as a person who could do just about anything you set your mind to." I respected Harvey, so I believed him. I looked at myself through his eyes, saw myself as Harvey saw me. I decided that if I could do anything I set my mind to, I'd do what I had always wanted to do. I became a full-time, working writer.

Now—eight books, fifty short stories, and a dozen years later—I travel this country and others, talking to students on behalf of the Pay-It-Forward Foundation.

I've delivered a message to more than 50,000 students so far, ranging from first grade through college, but usually middle and high school. The message is simple: I tell them they are powerful. That they are just as capable as adults, if not more so, at seeing the world for what it is. I tell them they'll be running the world soon, but they don't have to wait to make an impact. I don't just talk to them, though. I also get them talking, and I listen. They always seem surprised.

I tell them they can change the world with simple acts of kindness.

Do they believe me? That's hard to say. Often they go home and tell their parents what they heard. Sometimes they come up and shake my hand afterward. Sometimes they write to me to thank me for something I said. Not often, but sometimes.

I don't know if this is a message of hope that can change the direction of one of these kids. But even if it only reaches one in 25,000, then the effort may well have saved a life. Because, make no mistake about it, alienation is a life-or-death issue. Somehow, much as we hate it, we live in a world where kids commit suicide, or bring guns to school and take the lives of others. Such acts of desperation can, I firmly believe, only spring from an atmosphere of complete hopelessness. Where the slightest wisp of hope exists, we humans hold out for something better, even if it seems it will take a miracle.

So, what can we say to instill hope in those who need it most?

Sometimes I think it's not even so much what you say to a young person who respects you, but simply the fact that you took the time to listen and respond. It makes them feel visible, something I could have used while growing up. It makes them feel that at least one person thinks they are worth the effort and the time.

Admittedly, there is a challenge involved in delivering the words of hope that will turn a life around. The challenge is, quite simply, that nobody knows exactly what they are. But it seems to help if the words acknowledge humanity and the universality of emotions, if they're not sugar-coated, and if they come from the gut, preferably by people who walk the way they talk.

Whatever you think the right words are, the point remains that with the stakes so high, the last thing we can afford is to say nothing at all.

Forever yours,

Catherine Ryan Hyde

I am just writing to say that Speak *is probably the most wonderful book that I have ever read because you touched my soul with your writing. I read it front to back at least four times in succession at the beginning of this school year and have used it as an escape—until I finally got my voice back this year. Thank you. Your book took me back to my freshman year in high school (I'm now a junior), right down to the worst part of it. The guy who did it was much older than me, but because he was my best friend's older brother, my parents let me go out with him. At first, he swept me off my feet because of his looks and his build. I have since realized that he messed with me because someone closer to his own age might not have frozen like I did when "it" happened. I was in shock, and I didn't know what to do.*

Your book made me laugh and it made me cry; it made me feel; it made me talk. Thank you. The two years before reading it, I sulked, stopped eating, began to do crazy things, and convinced myself that cutting myself would ease the pain. I just wanted everyone to leave me alone. I convinced myself that I had nothing to live for; I just wanted to die. I have nasty scars that will never ever let me forget the "beast" who did it to me, but the scars also remind me that the most important word I have is "No" and that I have to learn to use it no matter how tough the situation. To make a long story short, after I got my voice back, I was the one who called the police on him. He is now in jail, and my best friend and her family are getting counseling. Me, too.

For most of my high school experience, I have hated men and have regarded them as my enemy. It didn't matter who they were either—the man at the food store, a male teacher, even my father. If one of them brushed up against me, I'd want to shriek. Speak made me realize that you can't bottle things inside because it will ruin who you are as a person and cause emotional pain for you and for others, even your best friends and family. When it happened, I didn't even tell my best friend and it was really hard seeing him when I spent the night at her house.

I noticed that Melinda and her parents didn't communicate very well, and it was negatively affecting everyone. Now that I've begun talking to mine, I feel much closer to them, including my father. I actually trust people now. Since reading your book after I told, I have a new respect for my-self that even the professionals have not been able to give me. I feel empowered, because I knew after reading it that I was not alone, and that I could be happy again. I got the courage that Melinda demonstrated.

Before I close, I have a question for you. What kept Melinda going on? I mean, she suffered so much for so long and yet she still chose to live her life. Why? In closing, I want to personally thank you for writing a book that helped me so much in my life. I might not be here if not for you.

Sincerely,
Debbie

DEAR DEBBIE,

Thank you very much for your kind letter. I'm happy that you enjoyed my book. I am honored that you trusted me enough to tell me what happened to you.

Your story . . . your story made me cry. I am so, so, sorry for everything you've suffered. And I am proud of you for having the strength to speak up and hold the guy who raped you accountable for his crime.

Nobody deserves to be raped.

Your experience is, sadly, a common one. It's usually a younger girl and an older guy, someone she trusts and is romantically interested in. Younger girls who don't have much dating experience are a favorite target of rapists. And let's be clear—rape is rape. It doesn't matter if you're on a date with your boyfriend or if he's a relative or a stranger. Anybody who does anything sexual with you without your permission is committing a serious crime. (And you have to be straight—no drugs or alcohol—in order to give permission!)

Everything you went through is normal. Lots of girls

who have been sexually assaulted have a hard time talking about it. They try to hide from their feelings and memories. They want to run away from the pain.

Pain is sneaky. It keeps showing up, no matter how hard you try to ignore it. If you don't deal with it, it poisons you. It comes out in unhealthy ways, either through physical illness or unwanted behaviors. That's what happened to you: the "crazy things" you did, the eating disorder, and the cutting. That was all the pain of your assault leaking out. So many girls go through this. They blame themselves for what happened. They begin to hate themselves. They sink into confusion and depression. In a way, they let the rapist hurt them over and over again, only this time, he's damaging their souls.

Thank goodness you did the right thing. You struggled for a while, but then *you* dealt with the pain head-on. *You* spoke up. That's how you heal. That's how you take charge of your life. That's how you win.

Here is a hard fact: we have very little control over what happens to us. Sometimes bad things happen. But there is good news, too. We have almost total control over how we react to what happens to us.

When you took control, when you spoke up and confronted your attacker and your painful memories, you got your life back. You are my hero.

Don't be ashamed of your scars, Debbie. Everybody has them. Some are on the inside; some are on the outside. Your scars will remind you of the long path you walked to become whole again. Whenever things get tough, you'll look at them and remember the lessons you learned on this path. You'll find good people to share the pain with. You'll stay healthy and strong. You will make the world a better place.

You asked how Melinda kept going on despite her suffering. She has the Gift. We all have the Gift. It is hidden deep inside us: the spark of life and love that refuses to be blown out, no matter how bad things get.

We are all Melinda. Her journey is ours. Sometimes a horrible thing like being raped can show you who you are, what you're made of. I think this happened to you. You found out how strong you are, and how good.

Thank you again for letting me know how much my

book helped you. I have heard that from a lot of readers. Writing the book helped me let out some of my pain, too. Sharing stories is the best way I know to share the Gift.

Bless you for having the courage to speak.

Bookishly yours,

Laurie Halse Anderson

DEAR MRS. SANDY ASHER,

Hi. I am thirteen and a half years old and so far I have read two of your books, Just Like Jenny and Everything Is Not Enough. Both are good books and both are a lot like my life and that's why I'm writing. Not only do I have a friend named Jenny, but my name is Sandy like yours and my last name also begins with an "A" like yours. In some ways I have problems like Stephanie because I feel I can't talk to anyone about them.

I have the same kind of dad that Michael has in Everything Is Not Enough. My parents believe that a person can live a happy life without friends. We live on a farm and I went without one friend for almost four years. I used to get so lonely that I would cry. Books were my comfort then and I guess they still are now or I wouldn't be writing to you. I'm so glad that at least someone agrees with me that friends are a big part in a person's life.

Last summer, I became friends with Jenny when she and I took a jazz class together. We had the best time of our lives *and laughed at everything. She is still my best friend, but I don't know about her anymore. It's like there's a barrier between us. I know that she cares about me, but she won't tell me what's going on inside of her and when I try to talk to her it gets all messed up. My problem is describing my feelings accurately. I get nervous and I make mistakes so I can't seem to get my feelings across. We promised we would be best friends forever. I don't want to force my friendship on her if she really doesn't like me, but it's so hard to tell. Even though our relationship has been strained, I know she cares or she would have moved into a higher level of English class when she had the chance. I heard she stayed because she wanted to be in the same class as me, but these last six months have been terrible. I have tried everything to be nice to her, even inviting her to do stuff and trying to hide when I feel upset so she doesn't see it. I bought a birthday present for her but she dumped it in the trash. The next week she was all bubbly and sweet and told me I had a really big heart and thanked me for the present. Then the next week she ignored me completely as though I didn't exist. It keeps going back and forth like that.*

I hate to feel jealous, but whenever I see Jenny she's al-

ways surrounded by a crowd and looks so happy. She is beautiful, funny, popular, and has a nice boyfriend and a dad who buys her anything she wants. When I tried to talk to my mom about all of this, she just said a "perfect person" still has problems and for me "to let her go" and "to move on." So what did I do? I ran when I saw her at the mall and felt so ashamed that I did that. I might just be being paranoid, but I really have tried to keep my end of the bargain by still keeping her as my best friend. Now I'm also scared of losing my other friends, really scared, even though the three of them don't mean half as much to me as Jenny. Please, please, help me. Jenny and I were once such good friends. I don't know what happened. I just can't seem to "move on" or "let go" as my mom says to do. She just doesn't understand.

I wish all of them, especially Jenny, could see how they hurt me. I just smile—it's all I can do—but I really want to cry. No doubt I'm being too sensitive, but every week I can feel that barrier and it's very real. Oh, please, please, help me.

Meanwhile, I feel guilty because I am so upset over Jenny that I'm not very sensitive to my dad right now. His brother, my uncle Jon, is in jail and he has to get the death penalty. My dad can't seem to move on either and none of us can stop thinking about what's going to happen to him. I know I will miss Uncle Jon when he finally gets the death penalty because I do now. I know I still love him even though he did a really bad thing.

I am sorry if I've inconvenienced you in any way, but thank you for reading this letter. Please write me back and help me if you can.

Hurting in Iowa,
Sandy

DEAR SANDY,

Thank you very much for your letter and for your kind words about my books *Just Like Jenny* and *Everything Is Not Enough.* I'm so glad you enjoyed reading them.

You and I have a lot more in common than first names and last initials! I spent a great deal of time in middle school (it was called "junior high" back then) and in high school believing that I had no friends at all. I, too, had trouble sharing my feelings, so I spent most of my school time keeping to myself and feeling gloomy about that. Books were—and still are!—a great comfort, as you know.

Like you, I did find friends and a lot of fun at my dance classes. I felt like a different person there, and also at theaters, where I loved rehearsing and performing in plays. You say you and your friend Jenny had the best time of your lives at your jazz class, and that you laughed at everything. I know exactly what you mean!

I realize now that I couldn't have been two different people back then—the laughing one and the lonely one—and neither are you. The friend that Jenny enjoyed so much in jazz class is still a big part of who you are. I think the difference may lie in how much of ourselves we choose to share with others. It does seem to be easier to be open and generous when we're involved in an activity we truly enjoy, so it's important to put down the books now and then and find those outside activities.

But there's more. The "barrier" you talk about can be raised or lowered from either side. Your mom says even a "perfect person" still has problems, and my mom used to say, "If only you could see yourself as others see you." You know what? They're both right! You mention in your letter that you wish Jenny and your other friends could realize how they hurt you, but you just smile when you want to cry. Maybe they're doing the same thing!

Looking back at my school years, I realize now that there were probably plenty of people who felt as shy and lonely as I did. Maybe some of them even wished they could be my friends but didn't know how to approach me, and I suspect it didn't help one bit that I looked so glum much of the time. Maybe some of them thought it was their fault!

There is nothing I can do about those days, but now, when I go into a situation where I feel shy and afraid no one will like me (yes, that still happens), I immediately look around for someone else who looks like he or she could use a friend—and I give that person a chance to be *mine.* Awkward though I may feel, I make myself go over and start a conversation. I ask a few questions and try to find something we have in common to chat about, even if it's just the weather, or our pets, or the food we're being served. Instead of worrying about how I feel, I concentrate on what this potential new friend is saying and how he or she might be feeling. It's not easy! It takes practice, but I'm getting better at it. And the more I focus on helping the other person feel comfortable, the less "messed up" I feel when it's my turn to talk.

Try it! In fact, you might want to try it on Jenny. Isn't it possible she misses the good times you shared and is wondering why you're hiding? After all, you're the one who ran away at the mall. Could it have made her feel you didn't want to be with her? I can't help but wonder about that birthday present you say she "dumped in the trash." Did you see her do that, or did someone else tell you about it? And was it the present that got thrown away, or just the wrapping paper and box? The reason I ask those questions is because Jenny *did* thank you for the present. She also promised to be your best friend, so she must have wanted to stay close to you. Think about it: are you giving her every chance to do that?

There must be a moment when you can catch her without the crowd and the boyfriend. When that moment comes, instead of trying to tell her how you feel, ask her how things are going for *her*! And truly *listen*. Accept as much as she can tell you, but don't pry for more. You know yourself what it's like not to be able to say everything you want to say. By listening and not judging, you can let Jenny know that whatever she tells you—or chooses *not* to tell you—you're still there for her. That's the best way to insure that she'll be there for you as well.

And while you're at it, take a good, long look at those three other friends of yours. You say you're worried about losing them. Might they not be worried about losing *you*? Do they suspect you care more about Jenny than any of them? If so, it can't be a very happy feeling!

In my books, Stephanie and Michael are finally able to "move on" when they begin to understand the other person's point of view. Stephanie realizes that Jenny needs her just as much as she needs Jenny. Michael realizes that his dad wants to protect him because he has good reason to be afraid that Michael will get hurt. I can tell by your letter that you know you need to be sensitive to your own dad right now. You're both hurting terribly for your uncle Jon and for yourselves. That's something you have in common. As awful as it is, it can bring you closer to each other. *If you let it!* Just as barriers can be raised or lowered from either side, the walk across a bridge can begin at either end.

I've given you a lot to think about, Sandy. I hope it doesn't sound like a lecture from a know-it-all. It's not! I mean it when I say you and I have a lot in common. I know the feelings you're struggling with. That's why I write about them! It's easier to deal with them on the page than in real life, but I keep working at it both ways—and I keep making progress. I believe you will, too. Know why I'm so sure? Because you took the trouble to write to me about Jenny and your other friends and your mom and dad and your uncle Jon. You *care* about them, so you'll keep trying to work things out.

You're not "too sensitive." You're sensitive enough. You've got what it takes!

All my best,

Sandy Asher

Sandy Asher

I have been reading your novels since I was in the fifth grade, and it was funny how it all started. I truly believe that I was meant to read The Lost Years of Merlin when I nearly pulled down an entire shelf of books and was only able to catch one—this one. Since that time, I have read everything you have written, and have reread them many times, too. Now that I am a teenager, I am amazed at the numerous new messages I get with each reading. Perhaps it is because I am different now. The thing is, I have cancer.

I believe that it is nice to be able to relate to your past and not keep focused on the future because fate plays its own role to a certain extent. As for fate, I guess once again it has played its role in my life. It just so happens that my class has been assigned to write to our favorite author for a specific reason, which I will further explain later in this letter. You would be surprised at how many kids like to relate to people they look up to, and a lot of kids look up to authors. Because you happen to be my fa-

vorite author, I have chosen to write to you, and now you will see why.

While I was getting chemotherapy and was sick in bed, your novels were constant companions to me. In particular, The Lost Years of Merlin and The Merlin Effect both held so much more symbolism for me while I was sick. Kate Gory's description of being mortal was extremely powerful and it got me to my soul. You see, I, too, was facing (and still am though I am now in remission) the ultimate mortal challenge—death! I guess I'm taking a long time to say that when I was really down and needed something to hold on to and believe in, your books were there for me when everyone else was asleep. I wanted you to know that, through your work, you have given me comfort.

Thank you for everything you have done for me.

Merlin lives,
Devon

DEAR DEVON,

Thanks for your wonderful letter! You are clearly an extraordinary young man.

Your letter ends with the line "Merlin lives." Yes, he does, Devon. In *you*. I really mean that. For whatever great things that Merlin accomplishes in those books, he does them because of the wondrous power he has down inside himself. And his power—his magic—is really not so different from yours.

Think about it. On the very first page of *The Lost Years of Merlin*, a half-drowned boy washes ashore. He has no home, no hope, and no memory at all. He doesn't even know his own name! But he does have that special *something* down inside—and that will enable him to become, one day, the mage of Camelot and the greatest wizard of all time.

Now, washing ashore isn't just a tough physical experience. It's also a metaphor, an image of what it feels like to be lost and alone and confused in life. Believe me, I have felt that way many times. Have you? I'm sure you have. So you understand exactly what Merlin felt like on that terrible day.

And yet, because of the inner hero inside yourself, you have found the strength to go on. You have stood up on that shore, brushed the sand off your arms and legs, taken a deep breath—and started all over again.

Just like Merlin.

You, too, have shown all the qualities of a hero. You, too, have amazing gifts down inside. And you, too, have a truly wonderful future ahead for yourself.

So, just as you said: Merlin lives!

Thanks so much for touching me with your magic.

My very best wishes to you,

T. A. Barron

T. A. Barron

Hi. My name is Bethany, and I'm a ninth grader at a high school in California. I just finished a book called Rules of the Road *that you wrote. I read it because I remembered you from last year and thought that maybe you would understand the problem I'm having now. I somehow feel connected to you. I know that sounds crazy, but let me explain.*

On the first day of the eighth grade, I went to second period, which happened to be photography. When I arrived at the large darkroom, I looked around at the people in my class and felt very out of place. There were four other girls in my class, and all of them were extremely popular. I'm not a dork, but I'm not all that popular either. When my teacher said to pair up and head over to the enlargers, I knew it was going to be a very long year when I was the only one without a partner. I thought about switching photo classes, but I had no reason other than feeling like an outsider. What was I supposed to do? Go up to my guidance counselor and ask her to take me out of my photo class because everyone in it was popular and I wasn't? Yeah right. Besides, I wanted to learn photography. It looked really cool.

Now, a year later, I've realized how silly I sounded. It sounds really corny and is an overused phrase, but people should like me for who I am. But at the time I could only think, "I'm not popular!" It seems really shallow now that I cared that much about it, but I did. Before I had never given friendship much thought. I had my circle of true friends and other friends besides them, but during photo class I felt different and out of place.

Then we got an assignment to read a book of our choice for English class, and I didn't know what to read so one of the librarians picked out one of your books—Thwonk. I didn't know what I thought it would be about, but I sure didn't expect it to be about a girl who was a photographer and in love with a popular guy she thought she couldn't have. Like A.J., I really liked this guy who turned out to be someone I didn't expect when I went out with him. I knew exactly how A.J. felt when she realized that she and Peter weren't the definition of love. A.J. knew that she had made the biggest mistake ever when she chose Peter over her real friends. A.J. was really lucky that she got all of her friends *back; unfortunately, I wasn't so lucky when I chose the guy I liked over my friends.*

Although A.J. thought that everything would be perfect after she found the stuffed Cupid and made her wishes, she realized she was wrong. She found out that every person who was popular didn't really like anyone else—popular or not. One day I was walking down to swim team practice with one of my friends—who is popular—and she told me how nice my best friends and I were. She said we weren't jealous of each other and didn't backstab each other. It was a relief for her to be with people who were friends and knew how to act that way. I realized at that moment just how right she and your book were. It doesn't matter how popular you are. The secret is to act like yourself and do what you think is right that really matters. I think I already knew that somehow, but I just didn't believe it or know how to put it into words. But now I do. I even became pretty good friends with all of the girls in my photography class before the year's end. With real friends, it doesn't matter if you're popular or not. To them, you're just you. Thank you so much, Mrs. Bauer, for not letting me forget that.

Then last month, my English teacher assigned Rules of

the Road *for my class this year. If I didn't know better, I'd swear she picked that book specifically for me. For whatever reason, Mrs. Bauer, your books really help me, but my problem this year is more serious. I know what it's like having a family member with a heavy drinking problem. My dad is an alcoholic. My mom had a talk with him a couple of years ago about how his drinking was going to influence me, but now they're divorced and his drinking has only gotten worse. I want to be the best daughter in the world, but nothing I do or say seems to help him. He's my dad, and I love him.*

I really like Jenna and how she deals with her problems. I know you wrote this book based on some of your real-life problems and I was wondering—not to be nosy or anything—if writing about your problems made you feel better. Your other book helped me so much. I'm hoping you can help me again.

Sincerely yours,
Bethany

DEAR BETHANY,

I want to thank you for your letter and for the honesty it took to write it. I understand a bit of what you're going through because my father was an alcoholic, too. It's such a difficult thing to see someone you love keep hurting themselves and those around them. For a long time I would hide from the truth—tell myself it wasn't so bad, tell myself if I could be a better daughter, student, whatever, that my dad would stop drinking. I know what it's like to take an adult's alcoholism on your shoulders. Living with alcoholism can make you feel unsure about all kinds of things. It's a heavy load, but one we are not meant to carry alone.

But it sounds to me like you've thought hard about your dad and how you want to respond to him in love. Sometimes we think that loving someone means we don't have any right to set up boundaries in the relationship. But Jenna in *Rules of the Road* found out how to love her dad and take care of herself at the same time. She learned all she could about the disease, and decided after much struggling that it had nothing to do with her. She learned to look at the part of her dad she didn't like—his drinking; his inconsistency—and see that that was not all there was to him. She learned to separate the good and the bad in their relationship. She was on her way, too, to understanding when the alcohol was in control of her father and how she needed to protect herself. We saw that happen in the scene when her father was driving drunk and she stopped the car. We saw it in the last scene where she told him the pain his drinking had caused her. She learned to stand tall—and I'm not just talking height here! She learned what you learned in photo class—to be herself and to like being herself in the process.

What I wanted to get across with *Rules of the Road* is that girls like Jenna, people like you and me, Bethany, have learned hard things because we were exposed to a loved one's drinking problem, but there is a silver lining to this stormy cloud. And that is, when you struggle through something very, very difficult, and you learn to overcome it, you become a much stronger person in the process. Great adversity can produce great strength and insight if we let it. That gives me such hope. And I want to encourage you that what you are going through is building powerful inner strength in you. How do I know that? The way you wrote your letter told me beyond a doubt. I encourage you, Bethany, to continue to use your writing to make sense of difficult things. There is something about emptying ourselves on paper that can bring remarkable courage and perspective.

I was so impressed by how you are able to see the different parts of your life and separate them into positives and negatives. You seem to have a firm grasp of the part you play in relationships and are able to turn difficult situations around (like with the girls in photo class) to make them positives. That is a life skill that many adults struggle to master.

Here's what I believe about alcoholism: First off, it's a *disease* that makes people do things they wouldn't normally do if they weren't drinking. There are millions of people who have overcome it, and there are millions more who have learned how to release themselves from the bad feelings that alcoholism can leave in relationships. Places like Al-Anon and Alateen are great places to talk about what it's like to have alcoholism in your family. If you don't have a trusted person to talk to about your dad's drinking and how it makes you feel, I would encourage you to ask a school counselor, your minister or rabbi, or a friend to help you find one. At the very least, look in the first page of your phone book for the number for an alcohol abuse hotline and call. Talking these things through is the most important step on the road to overcoming the hurt. I can tell from your letter that you are a young woman with great understanding of your feelings already. And that will take you a long, long way down this road.

I so related to the story you told me of your first day in eighth grade. I'm glad that *Thwonk* was able to help you put things in perspective. We seem to have a lot in common. I vividly remember feeling uncomfortable in school around the popular girls—it's one of the reasons that I wrote this story. I'm so impressed by how you worked through this experience. That label "popular" is filled with so much falsehood. I used to think it was the *only* acceptable thing to be. But you found out, like A.J., that it isn't always all it's cracked up to be. It's so natural to look at people who are popular, rich, or famous and think, "Boy, they have it all together. Their lives are perfect. If I just looked like them or dressed like them or whatever . . . I'd be happier." That kind of thinking can really make us forget the good things we have in life— like those true friends you mentioned.

I wish I'd had the experience you had in photo class when I was a teenager. Learning to be who you are and liking it is a wonderful achievement. I was always trying to be somebody that I wasn't—always trying to fit in places that weren't right for me. When I finally figured out I didn't need to do that, I was already an adult.

But do you know what? When I became a writer and began to write about the things I had struggled with as a teenager, I was amazed to see how many people have shared similar experiences and pain. I have a teenage daughter of my own, and one of the things I've taught her about people is that most people I know—probably all of them—have a broken place somewhere. That helps me remember that I'm not alone.

I wish you all good things, Bethany—love, wisdom, strength, and peace.

From one overcomer to another,

Joan Bauer

Joan Bauer

My name is Chad, and I just read two of your books, On My Honor *for class and* Face to Face *for extra credit. We had an assignment to write a letter to the author who wrote our favorite book. They are tied for first place!*

When I first got On My Honor, *I thought, "It's probably just another boring book," because I don't like reading most books. I liked this one, though, because it made me let out feelings inside me. I want to write young adult books like you do. I want to be able to write stories so friends my own age can read them and can understand things. I make up a lot of stories in my head, but when I try to write them down, I always get stuck. How come you started writing? Why did you write this story? Do you have something you feel guilty about like Joel? Is that why? Could you possibly write a sequel to* On My Honor, *explaining what happened to Joel as life went on? Did he ever get so he didn't feel so guilty? Sometimes I feel like everything is my fault, just like Joel.*

Face to Face *is great, too. The reason why I liked this one* so much is that it has a lot of deep feelings kids have when their parents divorce and remarry. People usually think parents are the only ones who have problems when the kids are probably having more problems. My dad and I have problems (my parents are divorced) so it helped me not to feel so alone. I wondered, after I read this book, if your parents are divorced or if you are divorced because your book has a lot of feeling in it.

Thank you for writing these books, and I hope you keep writing for the rest of your life.

Yours truly,
Chad

DEAR CHAD,

Thank you for your good letter. I'm glad that you enjoyed reading *On My Honor* and *Face to Face*. You might be interested to know that *On My Honor* is the only one of my books to be based on something that really happened. It didn't happen to me, but to a friend of mine when we were both about thirteen. Only the surfaces of the story come from the real incident, however. Most of the story, the part that makes you feel as though it is happening to you, is written from inside Joel's thoughts and feelings—and, of course, that is all imagined. That experience, looking out with someone else's eyes, hearing with his ears, thinking with his thoughts, is the most important one fiction can bring you. Usually my ideas don't come from real life. Or they may start from real life—a newspaper story, an incident that happens to me or to one of my friends, something odd one of my pets does—but from there the idea goes into my imagination and becomes something very different. What is essential, always, is that I must be able to find a central place where I can feel whatever it is that the main character feels. It is because of those strong feelings that my story, if it works, makes you feel strongly, too.

You asked if I will be writing a sequel to *On My Honor;* I don't believe I ever will, though even my editor has suggested that would be a good idea. I know the story ends with many unanswered questions, but I leave my stories open at the end very intentionally. If I answer all your questions and tie my stories up with a bow, then you can put them down and forget them. If there are still questions to be answered, then you carry the characters away in your heart . . . and the story goes on living. So I'll leave it to you to imagine what Joel did with the guilt he was still feeling at the end of the story. In fact, you can decide what you'd most like him to do with that guilt. The story and the characters belong to you now.

You asked if I have ever felt guilty the way Joel did in my story . . . and the way my friend must have in the real incident. I have, of course. And it's because of my own feelings that I wanted to write this story. I think everyone feels guilty at times, don't you? We feel guilty because we can't always live our lives perfectly. Sometimes we hurt people we care about, even when we are trying to do the right thing. If you think about it carefully, though, Joel shouldn't be taking responsibility for Tony's death. Joel made a bad choice when he went down to the river with Tony. But Tony made his own bad choices that day. Joel will have to live with his own choice, but he can't blame himself for Tony's choice, too, just as we can't blame ourselves for our parents' choices in a divorce. If we feel guilty about something we did that we shouldn't have done, the solution is to fix the wrong as best we can or at least to apologize. If we feel guilty about something that isn't our responsibility to start with, then we need to put the responsibility where it belongs.

I'm glad that *Face to Face* helped you know you are not alone in dealing with your parents' divorce or the problems with your father. Sometimes parents simply cannot be the parents their kids need, no matter how hard they try. And kids can't make themselves over into perfect kids who can fix things, because kids can never fix parents. So you have to do what Michael did, turn to someone who is willing and able to be there for you.

And by the way, you asked if I am divorced or if my parents were. My parents never divorced, and while I do happen to be divorced now, I wasn't when I wrote that novel. I didn't write it out of that kind of specific experience, but rather out of feelings that could be connected with divorce or many other kinds of experiences. Feelings of being alone, feelings of being at fault. If I've felt something, I can imagine many different kind of situations that might prompt those feelings.

You mentioned that you want to write young adult novels, too, and I'm glad to hear that you enjoy writing. I understand, though, when you say that you often get stuck on the stories you try to write. Stories are complex. I used to make up stories in my head, too, but I was an adult before I tried seriously to write them down. If you need help writing your stories, though, I suggest another book of mine called *What's Your Story? A Young Person's Guide to Writing Fiction*. I think you'll find it helps a lot.

Also, a suggestion . . . the best way to learn to write is to read. And read and read and read. Since you liked these two books of mine, you know that it's possible to find books that are right for you, so ask a teacher or librarian to help you find more books that you'll love. You aren't going to like every book you try. No book fits every single reader. But there are a lot more books out there that you will enjoy as much as you did these two. And I very much hope you will find them.

I hope the rest of your year in school is good, and I hope you find many more books by many different authors to read and enjoy.

Fondly,

Marion Dane Bauer

I just finished reading Life in the Fat Lane *like five minutes ago. I couldn't put it down and I cried forever. It was amazing that I could relate to so much of what was in it. Your book touched my heart. You captured all the feelings I have had in the past year, and I thank you for that. I thought I was alone and no one knew how I felt. Thank you so much.*

I would like to say I have read many books but not one that touched me in the way that this one did. It is now my favorite book and I can read it over and over again. You are one of the best authors I have ever read and I mean that. The book was sooooooo funny, but at the same time it made me think through a lot of things.

Many teenagers, including me, *stress out and obsess about their weight because of what society says you are supposed to be like. Okay. I admitted it! There. My name is Terrie, I'm thirteen years old, and I think I'm fat. Well, I am fat. My body has been through a lot of changes, and the whole thing has been both a mental and physical roller* coaster. I used to be super thin but then I gained eighty pounds in six months, and things began to change in my life, mostly taking turns for the worse.

At first, I was angry with Lara for complaining she gained a whole five or ten pounds. But when I found out she couldn't control it (like me), and how people treated her differently, it made me realize that we were just alike. People at my school changed the way they treated me and it just about killed me. I lost my spot on the cheerleading squad, but not until I was "benched" for everyone to see and make fun of me. I thought my whole world had ended. I was so depressed. I'm an eighth grader, and it is important to be thin at my age and almost every girl in my school weighs barely over 100 pounds. I wanted a way out and thought of killing myself two times!!!!

There's a clique at school, the "in crowd," who pick on people who they think are not "superior" or "cool." Your book made me realize that what they are doing to me (and others) is not right. Reading it helped me to understand what "cliques" can do to people's self-esteem and it made me think of what the "in crowd" was doing to me. I hope they read your book and realize the damage it does to people mentally, so they stop doing it. I hope they learn how a person's life can change so quickly without them having any control over it happening.

But your book also showed me that there is more to life than just looks. Even if I try my hardest to look good, I might never find true happiness. Image isn't everything. Now I believe that a person shouldn't try so hard to have a perfect image because everyone says you have to. It's what I want that's important, not what the world wants.

It taught me a lot about perfection and dedication and staying true to myself. I learned there is a difference between being fat and being worried about being fat. I noticed once or twice in the book where a teenage girl said, "I wish I could get just a little bit of anorexia" until she lost the weight she wanted. It grieves me to hear that, though I have said it many times myself. I would love to say that your book taught me to be OK with my weight but it didn't. It helped though.

I'd like to ask you some questions. Is this based on a true story of a person that you know? I might be wrong, but I felt like Lara was you. And I am really curious to know what happens at the end of the book. What about Jett? Did he ever learn to accept Lara's disorder? If you had to write a sequel,

*would you make Lara lose all of her weight or spend the rest
of her life in her new size? I know that Lara's weight isn't
the whole point of the book, but I was wondering how you
would write out Lara's future.*

*I'm not sure why I'm asking you all this, but I would love
to know what happens.*

Thanks for writing such a great book.

XOXOXO,
Terrie

DEAR TERRIE,

Thank *you* for writing such a great letter. I'm always
honored and amazed by the letters I receive in response
to my books, especially when the letter is as heartfelt
and personal as yours. I've gotten more mail about *Life
in the Fat Lane* than about anything else I have ever written; it seems to have struck a chord with a whole lot of
young women. So trust me on this, Terrie, you are definitely not alone.

I know all about the looks-ism thing, and completely sympathize with the minefield you've had to walk since you gained weight. When I read that you were a cheerleader who got benched for it, I wanted to personally go to your school and beat the crap out of whatever mental midget made this decision—and I am a nonviolent woman!

I am, however, also a realistic woman who lives in the real world. And in the real world, looks matter. Adults love to tell you that "beauty comes from within" and "it's what's on the inside that counts" and of course we all know these things are true, but it's not much comfort when you're at some dance with your skinny friends, all of whom get asked to dance, while you stand there all alone holding up the punch bowl.

Oh sure, you can say you don't care and dance with your friends and laugh really, really loud to show everyone what a really, really terrific time you're having. But it's mostly for show. When the curtain comes down, you go home and hug your pain to yourself in the dark where no one can see, because you feel so ashamed.

Or some variation on that.

It ticks me off beyond belief that thousands and thousands of girls go through that—internalize pop culture's "I'm fat, ergo I'm not okay" message. When I wrote *Life in the Fat Lane* I wanted to explore not just the psychology of what girls go through with their weight, but the sociology. It is my belief that there is a very wide weight range of what should be considered perfectly okay. Oh sure, you can be so skinny or so fat that it affects your health, you can't function, etc. But the girl who wears a size two is not *by definition* cuter than the girl who wears a size fourteen. There is nothing "wrong" with being larger. But there is something wrong with a culture that *tells* you there's something wrong with being larger.

Different eras, different cultures, have delineated different weights and body types for women as being the standard of beauty. In the fifties, Marilyn Monroe's size twelve/fourteen curves were the ideal. Today the kids at your school would call her a pig. In Latino and African-American cultures today, the emphasis is usually on curves rather than on being skinny. Are other eras, other cultures somehow "wrong" regarding what is beautiful? The idea is ludicrous.

So right now you're saying to yourself: Cherie, thanks for the lecture. But I have to live my life in the 'burbs, in the here and now, and no matter what I tell myself I *should* think, *I still want to be skinny!*

Believe it or not, Terrie, I think this is changing. As girls are encouraged to become more athletic, the emphasis is on what their bodies can accomplish, not how their bodies look. An athlete is the star of the show, instead of the anxious arm candy of someone else's.

Oh, I should mention here that I'm not athletic. Okay, so it doesn't apply to everyone.

In answer to some of your questions: No, Lara is not me. I was one of those theater kids who cringed at the very idea of beauty pageants. I had a circle of friends and usually had a boyfriend. I was also fat and I hated it. I remember a girl in middle school, Diane Levy, who waited in the hallway just inside the front doors of the school every day for me to enter, so that she could yell at the top of her lungs, "It's two-ton!" or some scintillating variation on that theme. I always slunk into school humiliated. I look back and feel so sad for the girl I was, who did not know she could or should stand up for herself. And here is the kicker to the story: *The girl who was belittling me every day was fatter than I was!!!*

Which means Diane Levy and I both needed to read *Life in the Fat Lane.* What happens to Lara after the end of the novel is for you to decide. I believe that whatever happens, she's stronger, braver, and wiser for having taken this journey. I like to think that I'm stronger, braver, and wiser for having written it, and it is my greatest hope that you are stronger, braver, and wiser for having read it.

Bottom line, Terrie: Real life is not middle school. And real life awaits you. Be the star of your show.

Stay in touch, okay?

All my best wishes,

Cherie Bennett

Cherie Bennett

I am writing to let you know that I really enjoyed the two books—Tangerine and Crusader—that you wrote and that I read. It is rare that I even like one of an author's books, let alone two!!! So, thanks for that. I even heard you had another book out that I will definitely get and read when I have time.

What Tangerine did for me is this: I learned that looking like or acting like a nerd doesn't mean a thing. It's who you are on the inside that counts. Before I read this book, I used to get really bothered by kids making fun of me for the way I act and the way I dress. At school, some kids call me "Osama," and they are not being nice when they say it. I used to just want to fit in and be like the rest of them but not anymore. Through Paul, I learned that it doesn't matter what other people think. It's what I think about myself that counts. Many people in my class just don't want to know me, and that's the way it is.

What Crusader did for me is this: I finally read a book

that showed a Muslim boy in a positive way. It seems like every time I read a book with a Muslim in it, the person is obsessed with fighting, is ruthless, or is "sick in the head" (like the girl in The Terrorist *by Caroline B. Cooney). Sometimes when I go to public places, I wonder if people look at me like I'm dangerous because of books like* The Terrorist, *movies like* The Siege *(with Denzel Washington) and, most of all, because of what happened on September 11, 2001. Like all Americans, my family and I think those attacks that day were a terrible thing.*

Crusader *also showed me that there are always two sides (or more) to practically everything. So, if you have time, I'd like to know more about the Crusades, especially information on the Arab side of the story.*

Thank you for your time,
Nima

DEAR NIMA,

Thank you for your letter. I am happy to hear that you liked *Tangerine* and *Crusader*. Yes, I do have another novel out, called *Story Time*. It's different from my first two books in that it is told by a third-person narrator, and it has a supernatural element. (It's set in a haunted library.) But it is similar to them in many ways, too. I hope you will like it.

You are right, of course, that the terrorist attacks in New York, Washington, and Pennsylvania on September 11 were "a terrible thing" for all Americans. I am troubled to think how much worse innocent Middle Eastern kids (or even kids who simply look Middle Eastern) are treated now.

I just finished a new novel titled *London Calling* that is set partially in the past, in the 1940s. At that time, American citizens of German, Italian, and Japanese descent were being beaten and insulted in their businesses and on the streets because of the actions of the German, Italian, and Japanese governments in World War II. It is a sad, recurring fact of human history that people lash out, out of frustration and ignorance, at the wrong targets. My wife's uncle experienced this as a boy in Vienna, Austria, when he and other Jewish Austrians suddenly became labeled as the enemy and pointed to as the reason why everything was wrong in the world. Unfortunately, the same thing still happens today.

People who scapegoat Arabs and Muslims are wrong to do so, and they should be ashamed of themselves. These terrorist attacks were crimes and should be treated as such. The criminals who committed them should be brought to justice. Hate crimes against innocent people are the worst possible reactions to what were, at their core, the very same thing—hate crimes against innocent people.

You asked me to recommend readings about the Crusades from the Arab point of view. [I would think this is because of comments made by that Muslim character, Sam, about how the people living in the Holy Land looked upon the Crusades not as a righteous action by God's own army, but as a murderous invasion by Europeans looking for loot.] I did a quick Web search and found two titles: *Arab Historians of the Crusades*, edited by Francesco Gabrieli (Dorset Press, 1989); and *The Crusades through Arab Eyes* by Amin Maalouf (Shocken Books, 1987). Both are available on Amazon.com. I haven't read them myself, but they look like they might give you the perspective that you are looking for.

While researching *Crusader*, I did read an article in *The Atlantic* magazine titled "The Roots of Muslim Rage." The article is rather dated now, but it still provides some valuable insights into why Arab and Muslim nations might resent the United States so much. The URL for this article is www.theatlantic.com/doc/prem/199009/muslim-rage.

I hope all Americans will be as concerned as you are about blind prejudice against innocent people. I hope we can all learn to respect the right of other people to have other viewpoints. If we do not, then these cycles of ignorance, prejudice, and violence will go on and on. I have a teenage daughter and a teenage son. I hope that their children and your children will not be fighting this same battle over the same issues because of the same ignorance. I'll sign off with a passage that is known to my generation but perhaps not to yours. It is by Pastor Niemoeler, a Protestant victim of the Holocaust:

First they came for the Jews and I did not speak out because I was not a Jew. Then they came for the communists and I did not speak out because I was not a communist. Then they came for the trade unionists and I did not speak out because I was not a trade unionist. Then they came for me, and there was no one left to speak out for me.

I am glad to hear that you are speaking out against the injustices that you see.

Yours sincerely,

Edward Bloor

Edward Bloor

Though I'm sure you've read many letters besides mine, I hope you'll find time to read this one for two reasons: First, I wanted to thank you for writing Notes for Another Life, *and second, to let you know that I have been depending on it heavily for guidance lately.*

You see, my boyfriend is really depressed and has already slit his wrist, though not seriously. I mean, it is serious that he cut himself, but the slit wasn't deep enough to kill him; it was, however, deep enough to make a scar.

Well, a friend of mine bought me your book for my birthday, and it came just in the nick of time. I, too, have come close to having heavy depressions. Last year, I was suicidal because I thought I was the only one with problems. Now that I am older (not very—I'm just fourteen), I can see that everyone else can get upset, too. It is comforting to notice that the people in your book have some of the same feelings as I do. So, if I get lost and don't know what to do, I will read your book again. I'll look to see how Wren held on to Kevin and tried to help him, and I'll understand her. I can look at Melanie and say that I'll never leave my boyfriend. When I don't know who I am anymore, I can always identify with the characters.

I want you to know that your book is much more than just a book; it is my life! I can only hope that my life will turn out as well as Kevin's seems to be heading. When I grow up enough to handle life fully, I want you to know that your book will not be gathering dust on my bookshelf. Instead, I will pass it on to someone else to help him or her cope with the world like you have helped me.

I haven't read your other books, but I plan on getting them soon. I also hope your time hasn't been wasted in reading this letter. Let me say again—thanks.

Sincerely,
Serena

DEAR SERENA,

I am touched by your letter. Your ability and willingness to express gratitude is beautiful. Sometimes I think we've all grown so accustomed to having what we want that our sense of gratitude is stunted. A graciously offered word of appreciation opens the hearts of two people, so I thank you for your letter.

Bless the friend who gave you a copy of *Notes for Another Life*! Writers are always glad when books and friendships are linked. I get such pleasure from recommending a book to a friend and finding out later how much it meant to her. Although reading (and writing) are solitary endeavors, they are also a way of sharing experience, of making the ground of friendship more fertile.

I'm glad my book has nurtured you. I sense your strength and deep resilience in your letter. In hard times, you are looking for ways to heal yourself. One of the ways we can do that is by recognizing that other people have similar feelings and problems even though their circumstances may be different. All through life, you will look for—and find—people by whose example you can model your behavior. Recognizing the problems others have and the successful ways they meet their challenges has helped me in my own life.

I've learned that success doesn't necessarily mean winning. Frequently, success is coping or surviving or living with a problem the best we can. Being healed doesn't always mean being cured. I think of my blind friend Georgia who sees with her ears, her hands, and her heart and is at peace with her life. I think of Margaret, a quadriplegic since high school, whose gentle presence inspires me to love my body and the daily labors I might otherwise find irritating.

Perhaps you know that Tom, the father in *Notes for Another Life*, is based on my own father, who suffered from a catatonic depressive state that began when I was ten years old. That kind of overwhelming fear—that darkness of the soul—is so debilitating and painful. At the time of my dad's illness, there wasn't much drug therapy available for him or any help for people struggling with a mentally ill family member, so we were pretty much on our own.

In Wren and Kevin, I hoped to portray my own feelings as a young person. To Wren, I gave my need to be perfect, to shield Mother from most of my own teenage problems because her life was so difficult already. To Kevin, I gave my fear that I would also be mentally ill. As a teenager, I didn't always see how things could evolve, how my difficulties with boyfriends, social life, with school in general, would change. Actually, they changed without my even having to do much about them. But like most young people, I lived on the edge of crisis most of the time and frequently thought I felt the beginnings of my dad's illness in myself.

To both Kevin and Wren, I gave my guilt at having caused my dad's problems. Since children inherently feel responsible for the world around them, I would have probably felt guilty even had I not heard one of Daddy's doctors say that family responsibilities were the cause of his initial breakdown. As kids, we seem to have an internal sense of power that is decimated by the time we're teenagers, when suddenly we feel more powerless than we really are.

I learned, as you are beginning to learn, that our stories keep on going. We suffer and recover, we love, we feel betrayed, we feel joy, we feel uncertain and fearful.

It's all part of the mix of life. Your life is bigger than a character in a book—it is richer, deeper, more complex—but from characters we can see new possibilities. We can find words to describe our own longings. Different books and characters will help you along the way. I think it was Victor Frankel who said that we discover who we are and what our mission is gradually, over time. I'm almost sixty years old now, and I'm still on that journey of discovery. I'm still changing and hopefully growing in positive ways. A famous writer, e. e. cummings, once said, "It takes courage to grow up and turn out to be who you really are." I don't know about the growing up part, but I do sense that my own personal journey inward is a search for my true self, a soul that is free to express and experience life in a most natural and fulfilling way. That's what I'm working toward.

I hope you'll be open to the changes and challenges ahead for you. You are, after all, the heroine of your own story. You will change your mind about many things. Be open to change. As much as you want to help your boyfriend, remember that he has his own story. His depression and attempted suicide are urgent pleas for help to which I hope his family is responding. Your main responsibility is to give pertinent information to his family, the school counselor, and health professionals even if you feel you are betraying his confidence. This is the time to take that risk because suicide means the story is over. There is no revision, no new revelation, no hero or heroine in that scenario.

Serena, although your letter expresses deep concerns about your circumstances, I also feel your passion for life. Your depression may well indicate the depth of your passion. Being passionate—feeling strongly and acting bravely—is a wonderful trait. Passion combined with your sense of gratitude, your willingness to search for answers to your questions, and your openness to literature as a tool for understanding point to a rich, full life for you. As a fellow traveler, I wish you high spirits for your journey and Godspeed along the way.

With all good wishes,

Sue Ellen Bridgers

Sue Ellen Bridgers

About two weeks ago my teacher gave me a book to read that you wrote called Chinese Handcuffs. *I don't read very many books, and I thought it was going to be boring. In fact, I don't read any books. But I started reading this book and it was so good I couldn't put it down. Only I don't mean it was good like it was fun or anything like that. I mean it was good because when I read it, I thought the author—that would be you—knew me. Some of the things that happened to Jen happened to me, only I didn't know they happened to anybody else. It was like she was my friend or something.*

When I first read the story and there wasn't a picture of you or anything, I thought you were a lady author because most of the Chrises I know are girls. Then I asked my teacher, and she told me you are a man and proved it because she showed me a picture of you that was in another book.

I have some questions to ask you, and I hope you will write me back and answer them. How could you write a story like this if you're a man? How would you know what it is like, especially the part where Jen says she goes away when it's happening to her? Do you know somebody this happened to? And how did you know the part about how mad she got at Dillon when he snuck the secret camera into her room and videotaped her stepfather doing it to her? And if you knew somebody who had something like that happen in real life, what would you tell her?

So I just wanted to thank you for writing a really good book. I hope you will write me back.

Jane

DEAR JANE,

Thanks for your good words about *Chinese Handcuffs*. It's always good to get feedback from thoughtful readers.

You're right. I'm not a lady author, and in this case I think it's a compliment that you thought so, so thank you for that, too.

You asked how I knew the same things about Jen that

you seem to know. I've worked for the past eight years as a child and family therapist at our community mental health center, dealing mostly with child abuse and neglect cases. That has brought me into contact with a great number of people who have endured what Jen endured. Though her particular story is fiction, in the sense that the *events* in the story didn't happen as written, all her responses come from what I have learned in this business. In other words, her responses are true responses to tough situations.

You asked what I would tell someone who has gone through the kind of sexual mistreatment Jen went through. I would tell them several things. First I would say, "You are not alone." Unfortunately many girls—and boys—have lived through the lies created by that kind of situation. The sad truth of the matter is that approximately one in four girls and one in six boys have been sexually violated in some way during their childhoods. Usually the person who does it is a family member or a "friend" of the family who also needs help. There are people out there who can help, and I would emphasize that it is more important that they know to get help in order to work through the pain the secrets create. It's not a fun process, but at least the abuse will stop and the pain becomes manageable.

Thank you again for taking time to give me your response to my book. It is appreciated.

Sincerely,

Chris Crutcher

Thank you for answering my letter. I've never written to an author before, and I was surprised when I got a letter back.

I have a question to ask you, and I want you to say no if you want to. Would it be all right if I wrote you once in a while to talk about some of the things I said in my last letter? You know, the stuff that happened to Jen in Chinese Handcuffs. I know you are a busy author and my teacher said you are still a counselor sometimes, but it is really hard to talk about this stuff to people here. Please feel free to tell me no if you don't have the time.

Your friend,
Jane

DEAR JANE,

You can write to me as much as you'd like, and I will write you back when I can. **But it will not take care of the business you need to take care of.** The kind of work you need to do can't be done through the mail. My advice is to find an adult—someone you trust—to help you. I'm guessing that the person who gave you *Chinese Handcuffs* gave it to you for a reason, particularly if it isn't a book the rest of your class is reading. Find out if your teacher read the book before she gave it to you. If so, you know she has the sensibilities to be respectful of the things the character went through and, therefore, can be respectful of your situation.

Please find an adult who can help you find the help you need. This is the kind of thing where *it is very important* to let people with experience give you guidance.

I would be happy to hear how you are doing. It takes a lot of courage to tell your story—a lot of courage to stand up for yourself. Now you need to find someone who appreciates that courage. There are a lot of good therapists out there trained to walk through this with you. At the very least, call the Abuse Hotline at 1-800-422-4453 and ask what to do.

What I would like for you to do is consider what I've said, then decide how to proceed. I would be more than happy to give you feedback and help with the decision-making process, but my experience tells me the work itself needs to be done face-to-face.

Sincerely,

Chris Crutcher

Hi. My name is Akmed, and I am in the eighth grade. We had to pick an author to study so I picked you. I thought your book The Watsons Go to Birmingham—1963 was going to be boring. To my surprise it wasn't. Your book really entertained me and got me fired up, especially at the end. It even kept me up some nights. But the one that's really gotten to me the most is Bud, Not Buddy. And that's why I'm writing.

Besides learning stuff about the Great Depression, I learned about the racism that existed between the white people and the black people. I got so mad when Bud and other African-American characters were treated unfairly simply because of their skin color. I was disgusted when the white Flint police officers burned down Hooverville and shot holes in the cooking pots so the black women and children had nowhere to sleep and no way to cook. I was outraged when I read the part about African-American boys having to watch out for Ku Klux Klan members at night. Thank goodness *that Lefty Lewis warned Bud about Owosso. I found out that Lefty Lewis was an actual person and that some people got hurt from jumping trains. Your book helped me understand why people live in orphanages and why people run away from their families. I'm lucky that I live with my mom, but she has a very rare disease and I often worry about her dying. Your book helped me realize that I don't need things of hers to remember her because I always carry her in my heart.*

My favorite part of the book was when Bud got out of the shed and got revenge on his mean foster brother by putting Todd's hand in warm water while he was sleeping. He didn't get back at him in a violent way; instead, he made him wet the bed and disgusted Mrs. Amos with a soaked mattress. I laughed for hours.

Bud didn't have much of an education, but he sure had a positive outlook on life and a hilarious sense of humor. I loved that he was always thinking and writing his observations in his rule book, Bud Caldwell's Rules and Things for Having a Funnier Life and Making a Better Liar Out of Yourself. "Rules and Things #8" was the funniest rule of them all. I love how you took a serious subject like racism and made it an uplifting one because of Bud's personality.

It made me feel empathy, and I wish it would do the same for anyone else who reads it.

Let me tell you something. I am not an ordinary kid. I'm Muslim. There's this ignorant man who lives in my neighborhood who is hard to ignore. He's done and said horrible and hateful things to my mom and me. Like Bud, I have developed many coping skills when I am really frightened. I play the piano when I'm in my house and try to turn that man's hatred into my personal strength.

I plan on reading Bucking the Sarge *next. It would be nice if you keep writing books so I don't have to read boring ones anymore. I promise to keep reading if you keep writing. Maybe one day I'll write a book and use my words to help create a world where everyone tolerates everyone. Is that why you became a writer? Is it something you always wanted to do? If you can, please answer the questions.*

Your inspired reader,
Akmed

DEAR AKMED,

Thank you very much for your thoughtful letter; you made my day! I don't think there's anything that is more musical to an author's ears than to hear that his or her book has helped a reader to learn or understand something. When I write, there are several things I hope for. First, I hope you have a good time while reading the book. As an author my job is to keep the reader turning pages, so I'm pleased you enjoyed both books.

The thing I hope for most, though, is that the reading makes you think. I hope that after you read the last page something about the book will stick with you. I hope the book will answer *some* questions for you; but more important, I hope it raises questions that you have to go elsewhere to answer. For example, I think I've done my job if you read *Bud, Not Buddy* and wonder what life during the Depression was really like for children his age. I've done my job if you're inspired to go read another book about the time or look in a magazine or newspaper to get a better idea of the problems Bud faced. From what you wrote I feel like I've done my job!

(In fact, Akmed, I'm thinking about going to someone and asking for a raise!)

As far as your ignorant neighbor is concerned, Akmed, the only advice I can offer is to stay strong. Know you're not alone. I find it both terrible and amazing that here in the twenty-first century we're still dealing with this nonsense. Sad as it seems, there appears to be something about certain people that makes them hate anyone who is not of their own race or religion or nationality or tribe. We have to feel sorry for them, but we also have to be on guard because in their ignorance they are capable of doing hateful and hurtful things. I like the fact that you channel your anger and pain into productive outlets, using his weaknesses to make yourself stronger. One of my favorite sayings is, "The best revenge is to lead a good life," and it sounds as if you are doing just that.

I'm sorry to hear about your mom's illness. That must be a terrible burden. But isn't it great that you can find some degree of comfort in the pages of a book? Your mother is obviously a good woman because she has raised a strong, intelligent, moral, sensitive son, something that is not easy to do. I hope you and your mother find strength and solace wherever you can: in your religion, in your everyday lives, within yourselves, and especially within each other.

I'm going to take you up on your deal. If you promise to keep reading, I promise to keep writing. (Actually I don't think there is anything that could stop either of us from doing these things, right?) Look around. There are many, many good authors. Talk to a teacher or librarian for tips on books; they are sort of like doctors for our souls. Instead of giving advice and prescriptions for illnesses in the form of medicine, they can give you advice and prescriptions in the form of books. And believe me, Akmed, a good book that really touches you will make you feel better than any pill. I say these things, but I have the suspicion you already know them. I'm not worried about you, young man. Keep using that head of yours and you'll be just fine.

Sincerely,

Christopher Paul Curtis

Three years ago, my stepfather killed my two little brothers and then committed suicide. I tell you this because I just finished reading Who Killed My Daughter? and it made me cry so much that my tears have smeared the book. I've always been afraid to ask this question but feel I can ask you. Why?

I also want you to know that your book probably saved my life. You see, I've been in a similar situation like Kait— I was getting into drugs, thanks to my old boyfriend. Although I love him, I do not love him or the drugs enough to put my mother through more heartache. Your story has made me think and think, and I pray that the people who killed Kaitlyn will be tried and convicted. I hope you do not hold all Vietnamese people in a bad light.

Sincerely,
Bi'nh

DEAR BI'NH,

The tragedy you have experienced is way beyond anything anyone ever should have to go through, much less somebody your age. I am so terribly sorry. You must be a very strong person to have endured such a dreadful event and managed to keep on going. That strength will serve you well as you get older and can share your strength with others who are facing their own tragedies. When you help such people, that will be your gift to your brothers—a way to give their short lives meaning. There's a term for that—it's called "keeping the faith."

I can't answer your question "Why?" I don't think anyone can. I have asked myself "Why?" a thousand times in regard to my own daughter's murder and come up with no answer. I see Kait sometimes in dreams, and she always is calm and smiling, as if she knows something I don't. I believe she will tell me sometime, but not on this earth plane.

I'm glad that Kait's story saved you from what could

have been a fatal mistake. From what you describe, you might well have ended up as she did. Kait did not use drugs herself, but the fact that her boyfriend and his associates were into illegal activities and she knew about those and was a threat to them put her at risk. I'm sure she didn't realize how dangerous this was until she tried to break away from the situation and discovered that it was too late. Thank God, in your case, you were able to get out in time.

No, of course, I don't hold all Vietnamese people in a bad light. There are many fine Vietnamese people. Kait's boyfriend and his group could have been any race or nationality. However, the fact that they were Vietnamese made Kait's murder harder to investigate, because there was no Asian gang unit in the area, and the local police were intimidated by the challenge of interrogating suspects whose language and customs were unfamiliar to them.

Bi'nh, I don't know what to say to you that will be of comfort. There are times when we simply have to swallow what life serves to us and move on to whatever comes next. It sounds as if you are doing a remarkable job of that. You have my utmost respect. I believe that you are one of those special people who will end up making this world a better place for all of us.

You and your family will be in my prayers.

Sincerely,

Lois Duncan

Lois Duncan

Today is a warm rainy day, and I just finished reread-ing your book Breaking Point *about twenty minutes ago. I just felt like I had to write to you. I'm a great lover of books. I have read more books than I could count in the past fourteen years of my life. I've read mostly the greats. You know the ones—Steinbeck, Hemingway, Dickens, and Shakespeare. I accidentally picked up one of your books and by the time I finished reading* Breaking Point, *I was astonished. I then found your other books and fin-ished those quickly, too.*

Your books are easy to read, but they still hold enough meaning to make an impact. Your books are so realistic that each one has made my spine tingle. In Breaking Point *I liked how everything didn't turn out okay, Paul was in jail, and it wasn't a fairy-tale happy-sappy ending. Not many people realize that you don't have to read just the classics to get a significant message. Thank you for giving me some-*

thing to think about. I think I need to reread your books sev-eral times.

In Breaking Point, I could truly relate to every single character in the book. I feel as if I was in Paul's shoes, and I have been in his shoes but not to the magnitude of violence (I'm certainly not like Paul in Breaking Point or Nick in Breathing Underwater). But I moved to a new school two years ago, and rumors flew about me. They hurt me but I didn't show that they did because I knew it would only cause more harassment. I've been cursed at, teased, mocked, sex-ually harassed, and called gay or fag. For these reasons, this book touched me deeply.

I've never been so touched by books like the ones you write. I plan to read more of your books. If they are any-thing like Breaking Point, Breathing Underwater, and Fade to Black, I MUST read them at any cost. Your books touched me in ways I can't explain. I look forward to read-ing more books by you. There are no words to truly express my gratitude for your books. From one person to another, I want to ask you a few questions. How can you deal with something you can't control? How do you make your books so realistic? Do you write from personal experience? Some of the situations in your book are unbelievably real.

I hope you answer me because Shakespeare and Steinbeck aren't around to ask. I hope this makes sense because I just started typing and didn't stop.

Thank you so much for reading this letter,
James

DEAR JAMES,

Thank you for your letter. You asked whether I write from personal experience. Yes, and no.

Yes, *Breaking Point* was written from personal experience because when I was in seventh grade, my family moved to a new state, a new school. I was very shy. I'd never really had to make friends because I'd had the same friends since kindergarten in my old school, which was very tiny. But when we moved to Florida, I realized I *couldn't* make friends. It didn't help that I had braces and glasses and zits and, and . . .

Anyway, I was always alone that first year, and I often got picked on and called names.

Just when I started making some friends (not very close ones, but at least people to sit with at lunch) in eighth grade, my parents decided to move me to yet another school, a smaller, private one, much like the school in *Breaking Point*. I can't blame them for thinking that would help. Unfortunately, a guy from my old school moved the same year. He was geeky, too, and I guess he thought he could take the geeky focus off himself by turning everyone against me, so again I was picked on and teased, but the second school was worse. Some of the things in *Breaking Point* actually did happen, including my being mooned by three jock guys in my class. The callousness of the school administration was real, too—when I complained about the mooning incident, and also about constant crank phone calls I got, I was told I was "barking up the wrong tree" in the case of the phone calls, and in the case of the mooning, I was told that it was a "very serious charge" and asked if I was "sure." Many people have told me that they don't think a school could be as bad as the one in *Breaking Point*, but

I know from personal experience that it can, and I know from my research and my mail that it still can. *Breaking Point* was a very difficult book for me to write because it meant going back there in my mind.

After my second year at that school, I begged my parents to move me back to public school to enroll in a magnet school program devoted to the arts. In eleventh grade, I made my first two friends in the state of Florida after four years of living there. Kevin, Laura, and I all went to college together and are still in touch to this day.

Breaking Point was *not* written from personal experience because I did not commit any desperate acts, as Paul or David did in the book (though I know some teens do). As a matter of fact, it is that difference between those who do desperate things and those who don't that made me want to write a book. During my middle school years, I turned my energies inward by reading and writing. In high school, I was into the performing arts, particularly music, and I spent all my time practicing, to the exclusion of everything else (including, unfortunately, my studies). Somehow, I realized that high school was a temporary experience. I knew that when I grew up, it would all be better; I'd be successful at something, and I'd *show them*. The character I relate to in *Breaking Point* is Binky because she, unlike Paul and David, realizes this, realizes it's all temporary b.s., and that high school coolness doesn't always equate with real-world success. I believe I got through it all because I channeled the anger I felt into my hopes and dreams for the future, by developing a strong interest in something else. Ironically, this is what also helped me make the friends I lacked.

The best way I know to deal with this type of situation is by realizing it is temporary, and a lot of people are going through it. What I didn't realize then, but realize now, is that most people aren't "popular" in high school. Most people feel alone at least some of the time. I wrote *Breaking Point* to tell a story, but I've found that it has given comfort to some teens who are going through what I went through as a kid. I think it's comforting to know that someone understands it and got through it by making good choices. *Breaking Point* is not my most popular book, but my mail tells me that there are a lot of teens out there who *need* to read the book, teens like I was. I also hope that teens who read *Breaking Point* will understand its underlying message: that it is okay to feel anger at people who torment you, but it is never okay to do what Paul did, to retaliate. I know Paul realized that in the end.

I am glad you have found *Breaking Point* because you sound like the person I wrote it for. Thank you for your letter. It's letters like this that make my job worthwhile.

Sincerely,

Alex Flinn

Alex Flinn

I would like to start off by saying that your book, Crossing Jordan, *was one of the best books that I have ever read. My seventh-grade class read it in English as a class book. It helped me learn more about discrimination and racism. I can relate to this book because many people in my class make fun of me because my nose is larger than most other kids'. They call me names like Pinocchio and Rudolph. I have had to deal with this since I was in fifth grade. There is barely a day that goes by when I don't get made fun of. Many times after school, I come home and start crying in my room. I just have all these built-up feelings inside and I would have to let them out. I try to ignore the bullies but it is very hard to because many of the kids who make fun of me are eighth graders and I am afraid that they will beat me up. That isn't that rare at the school that I attend. Your book helped me realize that all people in my school are not that mean, that maybe if I changed who I was friends with,* instead of trying to be cool by hanging out with people who hurt my feelings, I can hang out with people who accept me for who I am and not how I look. Like with Cassie's and Jemmie's friendship; it did not matter what they looked like, as long as they were happy. They did not care what other people thought about them because they knew that there was nothing wrong with their relationship. They also ended up changing the way Cassie's father looked at people with color.

It just surprises me why people think that it is cool to make fun of other people, because it isn't cool. It only makes you look like a jerk and that you do not care about other people. They do not really know how it feels to make fun of someone because usually the people who are making fun of other people are the popular kids. They just think that it is cool. Some days I wish that the bullies and the victims could switch places so that they would know how it feels. Hopefully that would help them stop making fun of people.

I just do not know why bullies do what they do. That is why I am writing this letter, to ask you a question. Why do *bullies make fun of other people and think it is cool? I would really appreciate it if I could get a response from you. It would mean a whole bunch to me. Thank you very much for spending your time to read my letter.*

Sincerely,
Billy

DEAR BILLY,

First, let me say that you are going to be fine. Everything in your letter lets me know that you get it. You clearly understand that it's wrong to bully other people, wrong to give anyone a hard time because they are different. You even identified one of the best ways to fend off bullies, which is to surround yourself with friends who like you for who you are. That said, when the name-calling and bullying are going on, you obviously still feel rotten. I understand exactly how you feel because I was the victim of the same kind of treatment. My problem wasn't my nose, it was everything else.

I was probably the least cool person to ever attend elementary or middle school. I was skinny and tall and had no idea what to wear that would help me fit in. The biggest influence on me was my mother, who was also clueless when it came to being cool in America. Her family emigrated from Italy, and while other mothers had their hair permed and wore makeup and cute out-fits, my mother wore her waist-length hair loose, went without makeup, and dressed in long, gathered skirts. The music in my house was usually opera. Try going into school and announcing that you love opera. She was a great mother—and a disastrous role model for me trying to fit in. Like you, I suffered, big-time. But maybe having gone through these experiences helped me write *Crossing Jordan*. I know firsthand what it's like to be shunned for just being who you are. How does this apply to you? I could have rejected my family's attitudes. But, I *chose* not to. You can't do much about your nose—except choose to control the way you feel about it. You can let the nose be important, or you can simply accept that you are who you are. Tell them to get over it. Life is much easier if you like yourself.

You ask why bullies do what they do. Easy—it makes them feel powerful. The bad news is, you may be doing something to help make them feel that way. They get stronger when it's obvious that you believe that they're right, that your nose *is* too big. And maybe it is, but does it really matter? Does your nose make you a bad person? The answer can't be yes. If it were, then being black could make you a bad person, or being Muslim, or being female, or being gay. Disliking you because your nose is big is just another form of prejudice. I can tell from your letter that you are smart and thoughtful. Ask yourself, on a scale of one to ten, how important is a big nose?

One more thing. I've always been sure that I was the hands-down least cool person to ever live through seventh grade. I can still see the popular kids in my class. Their faces are burned indelibly into my brain. One day at a conference I invited a large audience of teachers to do the same. I said, "Picture all the popular kids in your seventh-grade class. Take a good look, and if your face is in that picture raise your hand." Not one person raised their hand. Now, I know that in a room of 150 people there had to be a few who were popular in the seventh grade. The thing is, none of them saw themselves as popular. Chances are, none of those guys who are giving you trouble are 100 percent sure that they are popular either. Maybe they're a little worried about the size of their own noses, or maybe they're not that tall, or their clothes aren't so great.

Believe in yourself. Make friends who like you for who you are. One more thing—you mentioned that you were afraid of getting beaten up. If that's really a problem, turn them in. Tell a parent or a teacher. You can learn to ignore words but you don't ever have to put up with physical abuse. You have too much self-respect to let someone do that to you, and chances are you'll be sticking up for many more victims than just yourself. Do it. Bullies aren't as tough as they seem.

Your friend,

Adrian Fogelin

Adrian Fogelin

This is a fan letter. It may be just another fan letter for you, but it is the first one I have ever written. My name is Grace and I'm a young lesbian (almost sixteen, mind you). I just wanted to let you know that you've saved my life— really, and more than once. I thought it was important for me to attempt to explain how very much your book has touched my life in the hope that you continue to write the stories you do.

About three years ago, I was a hopelessly confused twelve-year-old girl who was trying to figure out what my feelings for other girls were. I just couldn't reconcile the image I had of "those horrible gay people" with the way I saw myself. Last year I found your book by chance in the library. Between my twelfth and fourteenth years, there was nothing and no one to tell me that my feelings and emotions weren't horrible and sick and that I wasn't a monster and alone. I have read lots of books with gay and bisexual characters and a lot

of books that tell you facts about homosexuality, but Annie
on My Mind *is the most real one I have ever read.*

*After I read your book, I cried tears of happiness when
you allowed Annie and Liza to love each other and I mean
really love each other. Finally, I could identify with another
person (I'm like Liza) who was not some stereotype. It is very
accurate and validating for someone in my situation. I noticed the label in the front is dedicated to the memory of
Matthew Shepard. More people, no matter what their sexual orientation, need to read it and let go of the homophobia and hatred they have inside. Last summer I had this job
where I would endure antigay taunts and come home and
read a few passages of* Annie *for comfort. I needed to know
that I wasn't alone.*

*I haven't even had a relationship yet but I know one
thing for sure. I want to do everything I can to fight for
everyone to have rights to love whoever they want, marry
whoever they want, and not be discriminated against. I had
to start with myself by first admitting that I am a lesbian
and that I am a good person. I have recently had a "first"
in my life, and what I consider to be a major step in my life
as a lesbian. I have come out at work. I started a new job at*

a veterinarian's office in January, and I decided that I would start out "out." I'm lucky that everyone is supportive, and it is such a relief not to feel the need to invent a heterosexual life. For the first time, I am really myself.

Before reading Annie on My Mind, I had never felt like a book spoke to "me" before. It was an unbelievable relief, and it convinced me that I wasn't destined to live a life of solitude and isolation. It is that feeling, that I can someday fall in love—that I will someday be happy—that made this book great for me. Someday, I can truly believe and it is okay to believe, there will be an Annie in my life. It gives me hope. Thank you for that.

Your biggest fan,
Grace

DEAR GRACE,

Yours is certainly not "just another fan letter"—it's a wonderful letter and I was very happy and touched to get it and to read your story. Thank you for saying such nice things about *Annie on My Mind*. I'm so glad that the book helped you, but I think you've also done a lot to help yourself, and I think you're very brave.

I smiled when I read that you "couldn't reconcile" your picture of "those horrible gay people" with your own sense of yourself, for many years ago when I was growing up, I had the same feeling! Back then, there weren't any books for kids about being gay (which is why I wrote *Annie*), and encyclopedias and the few adult books I found painted a grim picture that pretty much supported the idea that all gays are "horrible and sick," just as you found. But like you, despite what I read, I didn't think I was mentally ill or perverted.

Those years between twelve and fourteen must have been really rough for you. I'm so sorry you didn't find any helpful person to talk to or any friendly group like a gay-straight alliance (GSA) at school, where GLBTQ (gay, lesbian, bisexual, transgender, and questioning) kids can meet, along with their straight friends. In GSAs, kids can safely be honest about themselves and their feelings, and join in activities like youth Pride parades and celebrations of Gay History Month and Gay Pride Month, and can also organize, sponsor, and/or attend talks, films, conferences, and other events that deal honestly and accurately with homosexuality. But there aren't very many GSAs yet in middle schools, so there probably wasn't one for you to join during those hard years. There are many in high schools, though—perhaps your school even has one or could have one. An organization called GLSEN (Gay, Lesbian, & Straight Education Network—www.glsen.org) can help kids start GSAs, and there are a number of books now that list safe web resources for GLBTQ teens and give other guidance and information as well. One of the best recent ones, I think, is *GLBTQ: The Survival Guide for Queer and Questioning Teens* by Kelly Huegel.

But it sounds from your letter as if you've come

through that bad time with flying colors! Good for you for withstanding those antigay taunts and for wanting to fight for everyone's right to be free from discrimination and to love and marry whomever they want. You certainly took a huge and very brave step both for yourself and for that hate-free world when you came out at work! It feels great, doesn't it, not to have to hide who you really are? The more of us who can be honest about ourselves and show others that we're not monsters, the more people will understand who we really are. You're lucky that the folks at the vet's office are supportive. But please be careful, Grace; please, especially while you're still in your teens. Try to make sure that the people you come out to will be reasonably accepting before you come out to them, and that you're ready to handle a negative reaction from those people if you get it.

As you may know, there are antidiscrimination laws now in many cities and states, businesses and schools that apply to us as well as to other minorities. Psychiatrists and psychologists affirmed years ago that we aren't sick, and some religious groups now accept and welcome gay people; a few even approve of our getting married. Several other countries now allow gay people to marry legally, and so does one of our states—Massachusetts. All that makes me feel that despite the fact that yes, some people still do believe the worst of us, and yes, their voices are sometimes very loud, I think we're well on our way to a world in which people can love and marry whomever they want.

I can't resist adding another personal note here. My partner and I are lucky enough to live in Massachusetts, so we got legally married in June 2004! Even though our marriage is legal only in Massachusetts, I can't tell you how wonderful it was to see her family and mine, and our friends, witnessing our wedding and celebrating together. Since we'd already been living together for more than thirty years and had known each other for much longer, they all agreed that it was about time we were actually married!

You sound strong and bright, brave and determined, and I'm sure that you WILL find your Annie someday! Keep on believing in that, Grace, and believing in and striving for that discrimination-free world. With people like you working for it, I'm sure the dream of equality and acceptance that you and I and our GLBTQ brothers and sisters share will come true.

Thank you again for writing me and for telling me your courageous story.

Best wishes and good luck,

Nancy Garden

Nancy Garden

Hello. My name is Deidre, I am fourteen years old, and am in the eighth grade. I am writing to you because you seem to know how I feel. Two years ago my mother passed away (I was twelve at the time) from melanoma. Before she died, she gave me a book you wrote called You Shouldn't Have to Say Goodbye and said she thought it would help me accept the fact that she was not going to get well. My mom was right because my relationship with her was just like the one that Sarah had with her mother. It helped (I've read it a bunch of times) but I have good days and bad days, and now more bad days than good days. I know I'm not the only one without a mother but I still struggle with it, especially now.

During Christmas this year, I learned even more deeply what the cover said—"It's hard losing the person you love the most!" The year after Mom died, my dad moved us all to Florida to be near my grandparents. I had to say good-bye to all of my friends in Maine. That hurt, too, but not like losing my mom. Then at my new school, no one liked me except one person who was always there for me. His name was Michael, and I loved him a lot. Then something happened (a long story) and he shot himself. My best friend in the whole world killed himself, and I hate him for it. I don't understand how loving someone can hurt so bad. I love him, then hate him, love him, then hate him. I don't understand what I'm supposed to feel, or do, or think!!!!!

Can you tell me which of your books would be helpful to me? Can you tell me why you wrote them and if anything like this ever happened to you?

Sincerely,
Deidre

DEAR DEIDRE,

My heart aches for you in the loss of your beloved mother, and now your dear, dear friend. You have had so many, many losses, and you are so young to have to deal with all of this. So I'll level with you, and I'll take some words from my book *You Shouldn't Have to Say Goodbye* and tell you that it stinks. It really, really stinks to lose so much, so young.

But I can tell you this, too, Deidre: You are a gutsy, courageous young woman. You are not a whiner, nor do you give up. How do I know that? Because you wrote to me. Because you are looking for ways to help yourself. Because you are reading books and looking for hope and encouragement in them. You are not coming apart at the seams, though I bet there are times that you feel like doing just that. You are struggling, looking for answers, and you are, above all, continuing to live your life.

So how can I help you? I am not sure. But maybe I can help by simply telling you a bit about myself, and about why I write the kinds of books I write. You see, Deidre, I know a lot about loss. I've suffered lots of loss myself. Some of my losses were different from yours, very different. I was very sick when I was a little kid, and I spent a lot of time in hospitals when I was about six years old. In those days, parents couldn't stay with their children in the hospital, and so I was left alone, and was very, very scared. There was something wrong with my heart, and I wasn't allowed to run or walk—not even to get out of bed! Boy, was I lonely. And bored. And scared. Strange people kept poking me with needles, and taking out my blood, and I didn't know why or when the next one would come and do something mean to me. I was so scared and so alone, and I was there for a very, very long time. And every day, I lay in my bed, looking out the window, hoping, longing, to see my mother walking up the path to the hospital. Most days she did come. Some days, she didn't. (She had my three siblings to care for.) But those were sad days for me, and my biggest comfort came from books. (I'll tell you more about that in a minute.)

Then, when I was a young teenager, just about your age, another illness hit. This one was kind of spooky, far worse than something wrong with my heart. I would faint—at least, that's what my parents called it—and would awaken feeling terrified. There were big patches of time that had escaped from me. When I awakened from that "faint," I would have no memory at all of what had happened. I wouldn't know where I was or how I got there. Everything was forgotten. Even, for a few terrifying minutes, I could not remember my name, could not remember who I was. Talk about loss! I had lost big periods of time. I had lost my memory. My name. I had lost control of my body. (That's what happens when one has an epileptic seizure.) You see, I had epilepsy, though I didn't find that out till years later. My well-meaning parents, and they were well meaning, thought it was a kindness to hide that from me. So instead, I simply thought that I was going crazy. I mean, how else could I explain to myself that at times I couldn't even remember my own name?

And then, Deidre—this sounds like a soap opera, does it not? But I am going to tell you the most important loss of all. When I was a young married woman, I had a baby, a little girl, the most beautiful little girl in the world. I treasured her and loved her, just as I loved and treasured her two older brothers. And then one morning—it was a cold, raw kind of February morning—I awoke to find that my baby girl, asleep in her crib beside my bed, was dead. She had died in her sleep of an illness called Sudden Infant Death Syndrome (SIDS), but called at the time, crib death. There was no warning, no previous illness, not even a fever, not a cough, not anything. Just death. And how do you deal with an illness whose first symptom is death?

Deidre, I don't know how you dealt with the loss of your mother or of your friend, but if you are anything like me, I think you might have felt as I did: Stunned. Lost. Horrified. Confused. Angry. Depressed. Does any of this sound familiar to you? Were you furious? Are you furious? You have every right to be. But after the fury, the grieving, then something happens. If you really, really work at it, if you allow yourself to be in the pain and anger and really feel it all, you begin to be better. No, you don't "get over it." Nobody ever "gets over" a loss like this or like yours. But you do begin to get better. But note that I said, "*After* the pain and anger." Remember those words. Because you have to feel that pain, you have to feel that anger before you can get better. Some well-meaning persons (it's happened to me) will tell you to forget it, to not talk about it, to stop thinking about it. As if you could! You *need* to talk about it until—well, until you don't need to talk about it anymore! Does that make sense? And do you know how I did it? I did it by writing about it. No, I never wrote directly about all these losses in my life. Instead, I used fiction to convey the *feelings* I have and had. In other words, the things that happened in my books never really happened. But the feelings happened—oh, boy, did they!

So how are *you* to deal with the feelings and the loss? Nobody can really prescribe for another, but since you wrote to me, I assume it's all right to give some advice. (Adults are always trying to give advice, are we not? But I hope that this is an okay kind of advice.) First, you might want to do what I did and find someone you trust, and talk to him or her about all that has happened. I mean, an adult, maybe even a professional. There are people out there who are paid to listen. Sounds weird that people who are paid to listen can help, but it's true, and they do help. Helped me a lot! And then, find something that you love and engage yourself in it fully. What could it be? What do you love? Some kids take to sports: running, soccer, cheerleading. Others take to studying, mastering a foreign language. Or—and this works for me, and for many others—let the artist in you come out.

Artist? you may ask. Artist? Me? I'm not an artist. Ah, but you are. We all are. There is the creative self inside each of us, and it is in the creating that we heal ourselves. Maybe your art is singing. Maybe it is writing. Maybe it is dance—or even sports, as I said before, because sports can be an art, too. But find yourself that passion, and engage yourself fully.

Finally, I am going to tell you what helped me when I was your age. Books. Oh, books helped me so much. They were not only a place for me to escape, but they were a way for me to heal. They taught me that I was not alone. They taught me that others had lived through such times, and had survived. Remember I told you earlier about how books helped when I was in the hospital? Well, the book that saved my life, maybe really literally, was *The Secret Garden* by Frances Hodgson Burnett. In it, the main character is alone—her parents have died. (You could identify with that, I know.) She is brought to a strange house where she is cared for physically, but mostly lives alone among adults. She is so lonely, and kind of mean and angry. (I've felt that way a lot.) But then, one night, she follows a sound and finds, in the same house, a boy who is also sick, alone, frightened. And a bit of a big whiny pain! He is sick and in bed and can't walk—just as I was in the hospital. The two of them meet, and become the best of friends. (But they also fight a little bit, too.) I felt that *The Secret Garden* was written for me! It was about my life—being alone, finding someone like me who was also confined to bed. And then, oh, joy! He is able to walk and together, they discover a secret garden. To me, it was a secret garden of the soul. The place where two kids could go to play, rejoice, escape, and heal. Have you read that book? I think you might enjoy it.

So, Deidre, I have babbled on, telling you lots about me, and I am not at all sure that in the telling, I was able to help you. But I surely hope I could and did. And I hope something else, too: I truly think you can help others. With all you have experienced, with the wisdom I am sure you have gained, I think you could be a great help to others in need. Keep that in mind. Be happy. You deserve happiness! Laugh and play. And get on with that wonderful life with which you have been blessed.

I hope someday that I will see your name on your own book—or up on a marquee—or on the cover of a dance magazine or a sports magazine:

DEIDRE—THE STAR!
THE KID WHO OVERCAME IT ALL.

Love and blessings and all of that,

Patricia Hermes

Patricia Hermes

You should know that Melanie was my best friend. We didn't know each other that long because she just moved in with her dad last summer, but ever since, we were together almost all the time and we were always there for each other.

You probably noticed I said, "was," which is because Melanie died right after Christmas. Another thing you should know is that Melanie ended her own life by locking herself in the garage and letting the car run. I felt so bad when I heard she died that I punched the wall in my room and the hole is still there. If I could have stopped her, I would have, but she didn't tell me first. Sometimes I dream that I get there just in time.

The reason Melanie moved here in the first place was that her dad had gone to court to get her to come live with him because he was worried about her being too skinny and that her mom was addicted to drugs and had a new boyfriend and wasn't paying attention. Other girls at my school say Melanie was anorexic and made herself throw up, but I knew *her and she wasn't that bad. I think she killed her-self because her dad called her bird legs, which made her so mad, and said if she didn't start to eat he was going to send her to the nut farm so she killed herself. It's a long story and I don't want to bother you because I know you're very busy, but Melanie gave me some of her poems she wrote before she died and I really need to get them published. They are really good poems because Melanie was an awesome poet like you are. Can you tell me where I can get them published? If I send the poems to you can you get them published?*

Sincerely,
Derek

DEAR DEREK,

Wow. That must really hurt, to lose a good friend like Melanie. Sounds like her death left not only a hole in your wall, but a hole in your heart, too. People who choose suicide always leave so many questions scattered all over the place, it is hard for others to pick up the pieces and move on. It takes a lot of strength, and I know you have had to be very strong just to get through these last five months. I really admire your strength and your dedication to your friend. Anyone would be grateful to have a friend like you.

I'm sure you meant a lot to Melanie because she shared her poems with you. Poems are little pieces of the poet's heart and she must have trusted you completely to share her inner thoughts with you. Still, she may not have trusted you enough to talk to you about her eating disorder. Lots of times anorexics and bulimics spend a great deal of energy acting upbeat and cheery so that no one guesses their secret. It's weird because often the very fact they are starving themselves is a cry for attention. At the same time, if family and friends find out the truth about their unhealthy behavior, they might try to get the bulimic to stop—and deep down inside, she doesn't want to stop. It's like an addiction.

See, something you should know about me is that I understand about anorexia and bulimia. I struggled with those demons all through my twenties and was even hospitalized a couple of times. I started out dieting, thinking that if I were thinner, people would like me more, that I would be more lovable. Like Melanie, my mother drank too much and took too many pills. She had a screaming temper when she was using and I grew up thinking that if I bit my tongue and held my breath, I could control her temper. I know that sounds crazy, but I was a kid, what did I know? Anyway, I grew up believing that if I kept myself under strict controls, I could control things around me. This kind of thinking is a little like believing in the Easter Bunny. A person's supposed to grow out of it, which I finally did at about thirty. What can I say? I'm a slow learner.

When a person first starts to starve herself, she gets a little high. It's a giddy, silly feeling. She feels like she is in control of the world. That feeling leaves quickly because, frankly, starvation hurts. It hurts bad. So, she tries denying herself some more, hoping for the high feeling again. Problem is, if she really gets into it for any extended period of time, it starts to affect her brain and after that she can't think straight. The world closes in; it becomes the girl, her mirror, and her scale—and each of those is lying to her, telling her she is not good enough, not controlled enough. Like I said, it's a mind-altering addiction.

Try not to be mad at Melanie's dad. He probably didn't know, nor did Melanie, that there are places where she could have gone to get help. Not a "nut farm," but caring counselors and support groups that can really help people with eating disorders. Most parents don't know what to do with kids who have eating disorders and wind up punishing them or teasing them, which only makes the kid feel worse about herself. And when she feels bad about herself, she goes for that starvation high again. Sick, huh? Really sick.

It sounds to me like Melanie was sick. Not a bad person, not an uncaring person, not a cop-out. She was a good friend to you, but in a mind-altered state, she made a bad choice. Maybe she thought she didn't have any other choices. Of course she did—there are always other choices. But when your world narrows down to you and the mirror and you can't stand what you see in the mirror, life becomes a danger zone.

And now, here you are. Wishing you could have caught her just in time. My heart bleeds for you both. As

I said before, Derek, you are one strong young man. I know this has to be replaying itself over and over in your brain, but you are standing up to it and looking toward the future by wanting to share Melanie's poetry with the world. I think that is a beautiful plan.

I have an idea. Do you have access to a computer? Why don't you start an online journal? If you don't know how to do this, ask around; a friend or a librarian can help you out. Post Melanie's poems, her story, and your story online. Link up with other kids who have the same issues and share their stories. Talk to more grown-ups, maybe a counselor, your parents, or even Melanie's dad. Believe it or not, there are times when a grown-up can really make a positive difference. You don't need to tough this out on your own.

Writing has always been my lifeline. Writing poetry, talking to a counselor, and (most important) Al-Anon is what finally helped me start to live healthfully again and learn to like myself. When I am down, I tell myself to take two poems and call myself in the morning. Try writing about your feelings of loss and frustration and share with others as well as sharing Melanie's poems. Once when I was grieving over the death of a friend, my grandmother told me, "Let the dead care for the dead and the living take care of the living." At first I thought that was way harsh, but as time went on, I saw that she was right. You take care of you, Derek. That's the best thing a friend can do.

Please write again. I would love to hear how you are doing, because I know you're going to do great. Melanie's memory, her love and friendship, are going to heal that big hole in your heart. One day you'll just realize the hole is gone and what's left is the memory of your beautiful friendship.

With love and admiration,

Sara Holbrook

I'm calling you that because you signed your book A. C. LeMieux, and I feel funny calling you A.C. or Mrs. LeMieux even though my teacher said you were a lady. Why'd you sign it that way anyway?

I loved your book The T.V. Guidance Counselor. *I'll be honest. When I first saw the book, I thought it would be boring and put me to sleep. I have never liked a class before this and I hated reading, but I actually look forward to this class now because of your book. I never thought I would like a class or reading books but now I love reading. Your book was cool because the characters were mostly our own age, and I would love to read others that you have written for my age group. Oh yeah, I'm in middle school. I also wanted to tell you that the whole class loved it so it wasn't just me.*

I liked the part when Michael Madden tells his photography teacher why he wants to be in his class. He said he wanted to capture people's souls and this reminded me of myself. Michael Madden and I have a lot in common. My soul is searching for something but doesn't know what. I don't want to turn out like Michael's "red Corvette" dad or even my own father (he left us, too), and I definitely don't want to turn out like the T.V. Guidance Counselor even though I liked her enough but she was weird. I've seen homeless people who look crazy. They scare me but the T.V. Guidance Counselor didn't. She wasn't homeless but she acted that way. Did you do that on purpose? I never thought about people like that having a soul before. Why'd you have Michael take her picture only to give her soul back to her? I have to admit that I didn't get it entirely—but I sort of do. Everybody's got a soul and it's not right to mess up someone else's, like Michael did to Janey, Ricky did to Victoria, Michael's dad did to his family, and how my dad's doing it to us. I might not read TV Guide (I told you I hated reading before this book), but I watch a lot of TV just to forget that my dad is gone. Is that what happened to the T.V. Guidance Counselor? Did her dad leave her, too? Is that what will happen to me? I'm not going to jump off of a bridge like Ricky did. I know better and besides, there aren't any bridges by my house. But, I'm mad and glad that my dad left. I'm glad because I don't have to hear him yelling anymore, but now it's just my mom who yells even though she didn't used to. I don't have a job to go to like Michael so I just watch TV.

My other favorite part was when Michael went to Melissa's house, had dinner with her family, and then went upstairs to her room with TRUST. Does that really happen in real life? You know, kids being trusted to be alone upstairs in a girl's bedroom? I told my teacher that was fiction, not just the book. Even though my mom says she trusts me, there is no way she would let me have a girl alone in my bedroom. One other thing, you should have had Ricky go out with Victoria. They fight like they are married, so I thought they should see each other like boyfriend and girlfriend.

My last favorite part was Carl and Mr. Thumm's relationship. They were always nice to everybody, like when Carl gave the platter of food to Michael, and Mr. Thumm let Michael have store credit when he didn't have any money.

*They even included Michael when they went fishing, which
was a good thing, or Michael might have died when he
jumped off of the bridge.*

Well, that's all for now. I hope you answer my questions.

> *Sincerely and your friend,*
> *Jordan "J.T."*

DEAR FRIEND "J.T.,"

First of all, I really want to thank you for taking the
time to write and let me know how much you enjoyed
The T.V. Guidance Counselor. When I write a book, I
spend a lot of time in my own head by my own self (or
with my characters, anyway), but that's only half of the
equation. The other half is you. I always think of reading a book as an event involving two participants, writer
and reader, who somehow magically connect, a mind-to-
mind connection, in the pages of the book. I'm so glad
to "meet" you via the book.net connection.

You've asked a lot of deep questions in your letter,

and expressed a hope that I'll answer them all. Well, Jordan, I'll try. I hope you won't mind a long response, because once I get writing about things I care about, I tend to just keep going and going and . . . well, you get the idea!

There's a simple answer and a complex answer to your question about why I signed my book "A. C. LeMieux," the same name I chose to use on the cover. The simple answer has to do with trying to help this book reach as many readers as possible. I don't know if it's true or not, but some marketing studies have suggested that guys your age are less likely to pick up a book by a female author than a male one. (Do you think that's true?) Since *The T.V. Guidance Counselor* is written from the male perspective, or point-of-view, I didn't want that to be a factor. So I did what S. E. Hinton did with *The Outsiders* and just used my initials, to stay neutral. (A little biographical background—I have six brothers and no sisters, so to think like a guy while writing this book came pretty easily for me.)

The complex answer has to do with identity. F. Scott Fitzgerald once said, "Writers aren't exactly people . . .

They're a whole lot of people trying to be one person." (All the different characters in my books are like citizens of a country called "My Head," and they're all relatives—of mine!) When I write in a voice like Michael Madden's, or Boog Buglioni's in *Do Angels Sing the Blues?*, I feel like a different part of me is speaking, not the "Annie" that my brothers know, or the "Anne" that my friends know, or the "Mom" that my kids know. So it felt right to give that "me" a different name.

The identity issue has a lot to do with Michael's feeling of searching for something. Maybe another way to say it would be "searching for someone," namely himself. Michael got furious at Dr. Sherman when the psychiatrist advised him to look inside himself for the answers he was seeking, saying there was nothing in there. I think part of what he meant was that he couldn't find the "Michael" inside himself.

Identity is something that grows. Tiny kids depend on their parents (or caretakers), and their parents' interactions with them and reactions to them, to develop a sense of who they are. It's almost as if parents are mirrors, reflecting this tiny little person back to themselves, until the image takes hold inside. As a kid gets older, starts school, the number of mirrors increases, friends, enemies, teachers, each reflecting a message: "This is how I see you. This is who I think you are." And a kid will start to hold mirrors back to others, reflecting that message to them. Parents are really important mirrors while we're growing up. If a parent isn't there for some reason, or isn't able to provide a clear and positive mirror—it can be a lot harder to figure out who you are.

Part of Michael's inner struggle in the book had to do with sorting out the distorted mirrors his parents were holding up for each other, and realizing that he was allowed to form his own mirror (opinion and feelings) for each of them, have his relationship with each of them, separately. The other part was the task of creating his own mirror for himself, one with a true reflection.

Janey Riddley, the "T.V. Guidance Counselor," was actually modeled on a real person who used to come into the grocery store where I worked when I was in high school. I was as fascinated with this person as Michael was with Janey, and it wasn't until I was an adult that I realized the way she acted fit the description for a type of behavior called "autistic." Although Janey's body lived in the everyday world of social reality, a world where we interact with each other, her inner world was like a gated community of one; you could view her behaviors as "No Trespassing" signs. But they weren't signs she put up herself. According to *Webster's Dictionary*, the word "autistic" is an adjective describing "autism," which means "a state of mind characterized by daydreaming, hallucinations, and disregard of external reality." The symptoms of autism can be mild or very severe, or somewhere in between.

When Michael told his photography teacher, Mr. Dorio, that he wanted to capture people's souls with his camera, he was being kind of a wiseguy. I don't think he had any idea when he said it that it would turn out to be true in a certain sense. I believe that whenever we make a connection with another human being, whether it's a brief momentary connection, or one that turns into a relationship, we have the opportunity not only to absorb a part of another person's soul, but also to give them part of ours. I think this is how we help each other evolve, hopefully in a good direction, although it can work the other way, too.

I say we have the opportunity to share our souls, because you've probably realized by this time in your life that some people are able to relate well to other human beings better than others.

And I believe you're absolutely right when you say everybody's got a soul. I myself suspect our souls may be the most important part of who we are—and definitely connected with our hearts, and how we treat other people. Though Janey's soul might not be "visible" to the average person, she certainly acted as an important teacher to Michael, even if she didn't realize it.

One last detail about Janey and whether or not her father left her: When I write a book, I write out little biographies for each of my important characters. I imagined Janey as old enough that both her parents had died. And so that's why she lived with her sister.

I'm really sorry to hear that your dad left, even though there's probably a sense of relief that the fighting stopped. (Don't feel guilty that you feel glad about that part—and don't feel guilty about being mad at your dad. He's supposed to be the grown-up, and that means he better start figuring some things out.) Having your parents get divorced, or separated, is about one of the toughest things life can throw at you. Here you are, trying to grow your identity, which is your job as a kid, and they're supposed to be helping you in a calm and adult way, which is their job as parents. But a lot of times, calm and adult behavior flies out the window when divorce comes in the door. That puts a huge amount of pressure on you, to figure yourself and life out on your own, especially when the adults are losing it big-time. I really feel for you, because I went through the same thing when my parents got divorced. I remember thinking, just like Michael did, "So, what's the big deal? It happens all the time." But it is a big deal.

I was especially lucky, because I had some great teachers who went out of their way to help me figure some of the life stuff out until I could get a handle on things. I guess they held up a mirror that told me I was worth taking the extra time and making the extra effort for, even when I felt kind of worthless. With their encouragement, I started writing, and that was when I started to grow into myself. And then I realized that part of figuring out who you are is figuring out what you like to do.

You say you're watching a lot of TV these days. TV can be entertaining and relaxing, and even educational, but it can also be an escape, a way of tuning out from real life, which might slow you down in your search for that "something you don't know what it is." So try not to overdo it. (Same goes for video and computer games.) Being in middle school, you can't get a regular job yet, but maybe there's something you can do at this time, not only to earn some money, but to keep the current un-happiness at home from gluing your door to the world shut.

Well, Jordan "J.T.," I told you when my words get flowing on certain topics, I tend to keep going. I'll stop the words now, but please know that all my wishes for you keep going. You take good care of yourself.

Your friend,

Anne C. LeMieux

Anne C. LeMieux

DEAR MR. CHRIS LYNCH,

Clap clap clap. That was the sound of me in a dead silent room after I finished Slot Machine. *I really like that Elvin wasn't a typical kid with no problems. All the details helped me see it in my head, and the story helped me learn to be nicer to other kids. I truly don't like to read. I used to think that it was soooooooooooooooooooo boring. Well, that was before my teacher here in juvie made us read your books. Now I'm glad he made us read your books because after* Slot Machine, *I read* Who the Man. *It wasn't boring either, and I couldn't put this book down. Not only could I see it, but I felt like I was there in the background looking at the characters.*

I had to do a talk on Freewill. *Will was physically and emotionally trapped in his own little world from the things that happened to him in the past. From reading this book, I learned that no matter what kind of situation you're in, there is always a way out. Sometimes life isn't fair, but I have choices to make in what I do. I have a free will just like the* book says. My mind doesn't have to be the devil's playground, and I should make the best out of a bad situation. Listening to my peers rather than my parents is not the way to go.

Now I don't want to go outside even when we are allowed to. I'd rather just stay inside and read and write even though it is a beautiful day. I do more of what others wish, than myself, it seems to me. Maybe that's why I can relate to your stories. Now I just finished All the Old Haunts and I decided to write something myself. So, what are your old haunts? Girlfriends? Why do I think that some of the stories sound like the person wanted to die? Have you ever felt like that? What would you say to someone who did feel like that? Maybe this message is for me.

It stinks that books have endings. I was wondering if there are some things you wish you were told when you were a teenager that no one has ever told you to encourage you to write books. Also, what is your belief about life?

Your friend,
Johnny

DEAR JOHNNY,

I have to say, that was the first letter I ever got that had actual applause in it. Thanks for that, because that dead silent room in which you were reading is comparable to the dead silent room I have to work in all the time. Writing is a solitary task, meaning, if I am not alone and undisturbed I cannot get the job done. Meaning, feedback (applause!) from someone like you is precious.

It's good to know you are not alone, both physically and spiritually. I can assure you that spiritually, I was right there with you as a kid who did not like to read. I was a very, very reluctant reader as a young man, and it is remarkable that I wound up writing for a living. I never read a novel that wasn't assigned in class until I was in college. The only reading I went for in my younger days was books about sports heroes and World War II.

But that's okay. The thing is, I was finding my way, in my own way, as you are now. You locate the kinds of things you enjoy, then you build on that, until you find the path that is going to get you where you want to go in life. For me that path led from a book on General Patton to my books I write today for you. For you that path leads from the books I write (and I'm grateful for you finding me) to the limitless possibilities you'll find out there light-years beyond my stuff. It's a huge honor for me to think you'll someday look back from some high hill of your life, and perhaps remember my work fondly.

A writer's first task is not to be boring, so I seem to have passed your first test. Even better is the fact that you can relate to my characters. That's the goal for me, to have readers get the feeling that the events of the book are happening around them, and that they are right in there. The way you appear to understand Will so well in *Freewill* indicates to me that the book was a good match for you. You are correct—you have free will—and you are correct—you have alternatives no matter what scenario you find yourself in. One of the difficult aspects of growing up is that we don't have the experience to know the many different ways of taking on a tough situation. I feel too many times we are inclined to act in ways we see other kids act—either on the street or in movies, TV, video games. But those examples give a very limited view of the complicated range of the human mind and soul. It takes a great deal of living, through good and bad, to have the sophistication to make considered and rational choices for ourselves. That's why bending too freely to peer pressure is a dangerous system for making up your mind on something: the guy next to you very likely doesn't have any more experience or insight than you do.

It is all a process of getting to know yourself, and deciding what is best for yourself. The person best placed to do that is yourself. You will find much of your life is spent trying to resist doing what other people want you to do. Self-knowledge is the most useful gift you get from aging. When you know yourself, Johnny, you know better what will make you happy. Try not to let anyone else tell you what that is.

And now I'm going to spoil it by telling you what to

do! But since you asked, can I suggest that if it is a beautiful day, get yourself out there? There is a time for writing and a time for playing, and to become a good writer you have to have a life. Enjoy beautiful things, do exciting things, get scared, get thrilled, get hurt, get better. When the time is right, you will write about it all, and it will be well worth reading.

I can see where it might look like some of the characters in my short stories want to die. I don't think they do, though. Maybe it is possible that they think, for the time being, that that is what they want, but I believe they want something else. I believe that they want to *not* want to die. I believe they want things to feel better. And if I were a character in one of those stories I would tell them that things indeed will be better. Because that has been my experience. Whenever I have been at my lowest, things have always picked up—as long as I did not make them worse for myself.

It's about free will. I believe in it. I believe that bad times come to everyone. And when those bad times come we can choose to either punch our way out or to make things get worse. Many times, I have seen people make choices that make things worse. That comes from the inside, and we are not helpless to influence it.

I long ago concluded I will not be the author of my own downfall. I refuse to compose my own misery. Darkness comes to everybody, but you don't have to embrace it. The old haunts are all the people, places, events of your life that contribute to who you are now. It is perfectly fine to be haunted. I wouldn't have it any other way.

I wish when I was a teenager somebody had told me to relax and not be in such a hurry. I was anxious to grow up, and so didn't enjoy those years as much as I should have. As a writer, I would have liked somebody to tell me to learn to be myself. To learn to *sound* like myself. We spend too much time learning to sound like something else, and when we unlearn all that, that's when we are born as writers.

Finally, Johnny, don't worry that books have to end, because they don't. I see all my books as part of one larger work that just adds to all the rest and will never be finished. I don't believe books ever really lead you on to big answers. At their best, they simply lead you on to new questions.

Thanks for reading me, and for letting me know you are out there. Keep on reading and writing.

Cheers,

Chris Lynch

Hi. My name is Alphonia but you can call me Shawnda. I am a high school freshman in a teeny tiny school in the middle of nowhere but I used to live in Brooklyn. I recently finished your book Spellbound, which, by the way, helped me with my school research paper on ghetto life in the projects. I didn't want to read a book but decided to pick a "black" book and it happened to be yours. Your book captured the realness of the "ghettoness" in the projects. Since then, I got on the Internet and have read two more books of yours, too—Chill Wind and Twists and Turns.

My favorite part of Spellbound is when Aisha and Raven are waiting for Dell to come out of the office and Aisha gets smart with the assistant. I was on the floor crying. My favorite character in Twists and Turns is Keeba because her little sister Teesha treats her like my little sister does me. For example, Teesha treats Keeba like she's stupid and so does mine. I can also relate to Keeba's attitude and we are similar in the fact that Keeba was held back and so was I.

First, I wanted to thank you for writing something that allowed me to actually enjoy reading—it really is a first! Second, I don't normally read but your books have me hooked. You can officially say that I am a BIGGGGGG fan of yours now. I'd like to read more books by black authors. I know there are more and more African-American authors out there, and we need to support them by reading their books. Your books can teach a valuable lesson, like how to overcome life's obstacles. Not to be rude or anything, but I like reading about us blacks, especially blacks growing up in Brooklyn. Now I go to a school with a lot of whites, and they always come up to me asking dumb questions like "Is this ghetto?" or "Am I a gangsta?" People say I talk ghetto but all I know is I don't talk country.

So, third, I have a question. I understand you grew up in Brooklyn and now live in Paris and that's like me (sort of) moving from Brooklyn to this little country, very white town. I sometimes wonder if I'm going to make it.

> Your BIGGEST fan,
> Shawnda (aka Alphonia)

DEAR SHAWNDA,

First, let me thank you for writing. Whenever I hear from a reader I am thoroughly pleased, but your letter in particular arrived right on time because I was having a moment of doubt. You know how people are, Shawnda. When I say I gave up my lucrative career as a corporate lawyer to try to make it writing novels about black teenagers, they give me that "oh-you-done-messed-up-*real*-bad" look. The stack of unpaid bills on my desk seems to rustle in confirmation, and I also "wonder if I'm going to make it." Then I receive a letter from you—someone at "a teeny tiny school in the middle of nowhere"—that is full of appreciation and, more important, identification, and I know I made the right choice, and that I *will* make it. And so will you.

We are both Brooklyn girls on the move, our journeys having already taken us far from our roots to worlds that are unfamiliar and challenging. Challenge can sometimes be painful because it is not easy and requires stretching, but like a muscle, the stretch is always positive. At your age, I was an avid reader. At your age, you're a reluctant reader. But when you do read, you enjoy books about the lives of urban black teens. And I delight in writing those books. That is the first reason why you'll make it. Because you've already discovered an important truth—if you open yourself up to new experiences you will find pleasure in unexpected places.

You say you didn't want to read a book. But you ended up doing just that. Because you made the effort to find the kind of book you *did* want to read. Then you found another. Then another. (And I am so flattered that all three were mine! Yes, I definitely made the right choice.) From your letter it is clear that you will go on to read even more books, which is the second reason you'll make it. Reading teaches us about the world and about ourselves. The more you read, the more things will make sense and knowledge truly is power. For example, because you read *Twists and Turns* you know already that being held back in school doesn't mean you will be held back in life. Keeba finds a way to overcome that obstacle, and goes on to make something of her life.

You wonder if preferring to read books about black people is "rude." On the contrary, it is commendable at your age. Adolescence is a time when we ask basic questions about who we are and where we fit in the world around us. It is perfectly natural that your search for Self would begin with the most obvious representations of how you see yourself today—a black girl growing up in Brooklyn. Let me ask you this, Shawnda: Is it rude for white kids to read J. D. Salinger's *The Catcher in the Rye*? For Jewish kids to read Chaim Potok's *The Chosen*? For Asian-American kids to read Linda Sue Park's *A Single Shard*? No, no, and no. So by all means continue reading whatever books take you to places you want to go, be they inside or outside your Self. You may find with time that once you're comfy in that identity, you may want to go exploring. And much to your own surprise, and hopefully pleasure, you may find yourself curled up with one of the books I just mentioned.

The fact that you have even raised these issues brings

me to the third and final reason I know you will make it—your mind. Yours is full of doubt, curiosity, and wonder—the hallmarks of a truly intelligent person. You *already* made it, Shawnda, so just keep on keeping on.

YOUR biggest fan,

Janet McDonald aka Project Girl

My life stinks, but I just read the best book of my life and I wanted to thank you for writing Freak the Mighty. *My school librarian told me that you knew someone like Kevin. Is that true? How about Max? If you have never known anyone like him before, you do now. I'm just like Max for many reasons. My mom died and I miss her so much. I live with my stepfather because my "real" father is in prison. I hope he stays there because he had lots of drug problems and was abusive to my mother, but he tricked the court into letting him out early. He gets out in less than a month, and I hope he doesn't try anything.*

People say that I look like him. It's like the part in your book when Max is eating dinner at Kevin and Gwen's house and he's talking about how he looks like his father and doesn't like it. I don't like it either. He's found out where I live and has been writing me letters but I don't want to see him. Because of him, my classmates make fun of me and call me names. Because of him, my life stinks.

When I get older, I want to write a book about my life. Your book inspired me because now I know there are people out there like me. My favorite part is when they become "Freak the Mighty" because together they are nine feet tall and can walk high across the world.

> *Thanks for writing your book,*
> *Joshua*

DEAR JOSHUA,

I was delighted to receive your impressions of my novel *Freak the Mighty* and how it relates to your life. Your librarian is correct—I did know a real person who was the inspiration for the character of Kevin. Like Kevin he was unusually small and had various physical ailments. Like Kevin he had a brilliant, imaginative mind, an interest in science fiction, and a love for the Arthurian legends. And like Kevin he had a large friend who sometimes carried him around on his shoulders.

At the time I didn't know the big friend except by sight, so I was free to invent the character of Max and his scary-bad dad. A tiny part of Kenny "Killer" Kane was based on how frightened and helpless I felt when my own father was drinking heavily, and the world and life itself seemed out of control. Most of Killer Kane I made up, or based on a few violent, manipulative people I knew slightly. Since then, however, I've met quite a few kids who, like Max, have fathers in prison. A few, like you, have also lost their mothers, which makes life especially difficult, even if you're in a good place with a stepdad who has your best interests at heart.

Mom gone, Dad in prison. Could it be worse? Yes, actually, it could be worse. Much worse. It would be truly terrible if you clenched your heart like an angry fist and shut yourself off from the anguish and uncertainty you feel. Or if you took that anger and loss and used it to punish others. Or if you let yourself become numb to feelings and emotions and to the suffering of others.

The good news is you're not that kind of guy. You are your mother's precious son, and you know what is right and good and true in this world. Your mother made you, Joshua. She gave you a life that will live as long as you do and will someday be passed on to your own children. Let me tell you a secret: there's an amazing, mysterious, and wonderful part of your mom who will always be in your blood and bones, and the way your eyes look when you smile.

Meanwhile, it hurts; and some days it hurts really, really bad.

People talk about death and grieving as if it's an illness you get over. On the surface that might be true— the waves of physical, body-shaking grief fade away as time passes. But the fact is, you'll always miss your mother and wish she was there to see what's happening as you grow up and have your own life. That's what it is to be human, but you will eventually discover that the pain of living is more than compensated for by the joy it also contains. Even though it may not feel that way when the bad rain falls.

You think you look like your dad. Okay, maybe you do, but if you read about Max, and felt as he did about things, then you already know how unimportant the physical resemblance part is. You are not your face. You are yourself, a distinct person with your own ideas of how to conduct yourself, and good people will see that quality within you, and come to admire you.

Joshua, your life may stink right now, but you don't.

Okay, fine, but how do you get to the good part, the part that doesn't stink? You keep on choosing to do the right thing. You keep choosing to pay attention to the world around you and the people in it. You keep choosing to lose yourself in books. Which is, weirdly enough, also how you find yourself in books. I can't explain how that works, except to say keep reading and you'll find out.

Right now you have chosen not to have contact with your father, and I'm hoping that he will respect your decision and understand you need time to sort things out. Time to make good choices. Who knows, maybe someday you'll choose to see your father again. Maybe you'll even choose to forgive him for having put you in this difficult place. I eventually forgave my own father for those scary-bad drinking days, and we became family again.

Miracles can happen, although in real life they take an awful lot of hard work. Like that book you will someday write. It will take a lot of work, but I'm betting you're up to it.

Thanks for reading my book,

Rod Philbrick

I wish I could be talking to you in person rather than writing this letter. You see, I am currently in a youth facility in Texas, which is also a state prison that is home to 800 women and 4,000 men. Three of your novels—But What About Me, If You Loved Me, and Telling—really helped me understand some things. I've been able to bring "things" up in my therapeutic support group. I can identify with Erika and Lauren and have a sister who can now identify with them, too. My daughter can't, though, because she has Down syndrome.

Telling was the hardest for me to read, but it helped me to understand some things I was going through when I was eleven years old. The same thing that was happening to Cassie was happening to me, but I always thought it was my fault. If I had read the book then, maybe I might have had the courage to tell someone before it went too far. One of my friends in the facility has a friend who we told to read the book, and she was able to tell her mother before things got out of hand.

We feel good about that and you should, too, because you're the one who wrote the book. As for me, I am a teen mother who used to be a drug addict and was with an abusive partner for a long time. Now I'm in prison trying hard to turn things around, and your books have been a great inspiration to me because they give understanding to us girls out here.

My thirteen-year-old sister just got Detour for Emmy, *and she said she could relate to everything that happened to Emmy. She asked me to ask you if it was your intention that teenagers reading this book would realize that raising a child isn't as easy as many think it is. We were wondering what inspired you to write these books. We both wished we had read your books earlier because we think we could have done a better job keeping our legs closed.*

I just wanted you to know that you are doing a great job and to keep on writing. Thank you for giving me an interest in reading again and for helping me to make sense of some things.

Sincerely,
Gabriella

DEAR GABRIELLA,

Thank you for writing. It means a lot to me to know that my books have helped you understand some things, and also that your recommendation of *Telling* helped another friend talk to her mother "before things got out of hand." Books and stories can be great sources of strength and understanding, and I'm so glad that you're tapping into those sources. As you've already experienced, reading can change lives, and I'm honored that my books have rekindled your interest in reading.

In answer to you and your sister's questions, I was inspired to write these books when I was teaching English in an "alternative" high school in California. Many of my students had been through hard times—teen pregnancy, molestation, rape, partner abuse, you name it—someone or another of them had experienced it. Not many of them liked to read, and those who did wanted realistic fiction that dealt with life as *they* knew it. I couldn't find enough such books, so I decided to try writing one. *Telling* was the first, and when I saw the power of that story for my readers, I went on to *Detour for Emmy*. I now have eight books of realistic fiction published, and am presently at work on another. So that is the short version of what inspired me. If this were going to be a book, rather than a letter, I would go on and on about a variety of inspirations, some coming directly from teens I've known, some coming as gifts in dreams, some from letters such as yours, but most coming from experiences and places not easily identified.

My intention in writing *Detour for Emmy* was to tell a complex, realistic teen pregnancy story, and to tell it in a way that my readers would understand and relate to. When I start a book, I never set out to teach a lesson. But I know that if the story is well told, readers will connect with the characters, and through characters such as Emmy, and Jeff, and Erica, they may gain insights into their own lives. I'm reassured by letters I get regarding *Detour for Emmy* that it offers such insights to a variety of readers. For some, it gives them the determination to keep their legs closed and not become a mom before they're ready. For readers who are already pregnant, or who have babies, it helps them see that, as difficult as things are, it is still possible to put together a good life for themselves and their babies.

Gabriella, just from your letter I can tell that you care about others because you've passed my book on to someone it might help, you're reaching out to your "little" sister, and you've taken the time to write a letter of appreciation to me, someone you don't even know. All of this speaks of a generous spirit. I can also tell that you're taking an honest look at your life, and that you're not falling back on excuses. Your generosity and honesty bode well for your future, and I'm pulling for you.

If there is any one theme that runs through all of my books, it has to do with the strength and resilience of the human spirit. I don't consciously insert that theme. It is simply a reflection of life as I understand and experience it. My hope for you is that your strength and resilience will see you through these very difficult times, and that you will, through books and friendships and plain old hard work, rebuild your life.

My best regards to you and your daughter.

Stay strong,

Marilyn Reynolds

Marilyn Reynolds

P.S. You are very articulate. Have you ever thought of writing your own story? It would be a great gift to others, and the process might also be helpful to you.

Hi, my name is Riley and I am in the fifth grade. I want to tell you that my teacher read your book Choosing Up Sides in class. Why did you name the book Choosing Up Sides? I mean, it was a good book and all, and I liked it a lot. It's so good that I want to buy it and have you sign it. My best part was when Luke strikes out Skinny Latmann. It was all cool except for the end. It was sad.

At first I didn't know why the dad had to die. I wish that after his son saved him, his father and him would get close and spend time together and do things together like baseball. My teacher told me to look at the story again and try to think why you did that. She heard you talk before. It took me two days to think about it. Then I remembered about how my dad used to hit my mom. But he never hit me. They always would fight. Then we moved away. I did not want us to go. That was the worst time in my life. But now I know why my mom had to leave.

My dad doesn't hit my mom anymore because we moved.

I can relate to the book because I feel like the mom. My dad used to hit my mom so hard that I would sit in my room and cry all night. I never knew why he never hit me, but the book helped me figure it out a little. My mom would stand up to him, but I couldn't. When I started writing, I started to cry. I also want to thank you for writing this book 'cause it taught me a lot about life and told me without saying it. For instance, when "Pa" broke Luke's arm it told me what could have happened if we had stayed. Now I know why my mom left. I mean, I knew, but now I understand. When you write your next book I would like for you to remember this letter. What made you write this book anyway?

Your friend,
Riley

DEAR RILEY,

Thank you for your letter. You have a great gift for making connections and understanding how stories can relate to real life.

You asked me why I called the book *Choosing Up Sides*. One reason was the fact that life is full of choices. Often difficult ones. I think your mother made the right choice, though I'm sure it was difficult. So I hope you can use your gift of understanding to see why I made the tough choices I had to make in this story.

I know it's hard to feel much sympathy for a man who hits his son—or his wife. But it was something I had to do in order to write truthfully about "Pa" Bledsoe. The toughest part was the fact that I had to go back into my own childhood to do it.

When I was very young, my mother died. And my father, who deeply loved her, fell into a depression and began to drink heavily. After being left with four young children, my dad feared he would not be able to cope. I learned quite early that when a man drinks, he morphs into someone else. I didn't like that drinking man. I hated the late-night arguments that filled our house, the screaming, the breaking of furniture, and the many sleepless nights I would lie in bed praying for peace, praying that my father could see the pain he was causing, how he was harming his children with his tirades, and driving the housekeepers away. In the morning, sober again, my dad would return to being the gentle, loving soul I knew him to be. And sometimes it would last all day. But never all week. Before long, I'd see his car roll up the driveway, see him climb out drunk and belligerent, and I would disappear into my room.

I never went through what Luke did. My dad never hit me or anyone. And like Luke, deep down I knew he loved us all. As your father loves you. But we had no mother to swoop us away. And no place to go. Besides, I always held out hope that my dad would change. That on every day, not just some days, we could, as you write, "get close and spend time together and do things together like baseball." But the fact was, in one way or another, he'd "broken the arm"—or weakened the spirit—of all his children.

As time went on, my dad did coach our ball teams,

and we did have some great times. He even remarried. But he never stopped drinking. And on the days when he came drunk to my high school games, I shuddered as the other players laughed at "the crazy man down the foul line" yelling and whistling at the opposing team. Eventually, his second wife divorced him. His children grew up and moved away. And my dad retired into a dark and lonely house.

Then one day, my older brother called to say Dad was in the hospital, near death. He had given up. Deeply depressed, my dad had stopped eating, stopped taking his heart medication, and merely waited to die. After a week in the hospital, he had stabilized some. But we knew that if he was discharged and returned home, he'd fall into the same old pattern again. It was Thanksgiving Day. But instead of gathering together for a big family dinner, my older brother and I sat in a bare, green hospital room while I wrote out a note to the doctor.

And when I started writing, I started to cry.

I told the doctor that our father had been depressed for as long as we could remember. I told him that unless he was treated for depression, he would be right back here in no time. Or worse. We walked to the doctor's office in the next building and left the note on his desk.

That was six years ago.

Today, my dad is alive, upbeat, and sober. He is the father I had always wished for. He treats us well, with kindness and appreciation. We enjoy our visits and relish being entertained once again by his masterful storytelling.

Then, a few days ago, he told me something he'd never been able to say before. "The doctor showed me your letter," he said. Then his voice caught, but he seemed determined to speak. "You know, it could've gone either way." Now he spoke in a forced whisper. "Well, I'm grateful. To all of you. For all you did. And that—that you didn't give up on me."

Together, my brother and I were able to take the right action. And, unlike Luke, we were able to save our dad.

It could've gone either way.

Riley, there is a man out there who probably loves you deeply. He probably loves your mother, too. Someday he may be able to come to you both and say so. With actions and words.

Maybe not.

But until then, it's important that you and your mother are safe. And that you never give up on him.

That's why I wrote *Choosing Up Sides*.

Thanks for asking.

All best wishes,

John H. Ritter

I've been a fan of your books since my English teacher made us read The Dark Side of Nowhere. *Actually, she didn't really have to make us read it, because after I started, I would have read it anyway. Since then I've read a whole bunch more of your books. It's one of those other books that I'm really writing to you about. It's your book* What Daddy Did. *When I read it, I wasn't expecting it. Since a lot of your other books are kind of weird, I didn't think it would be so real.*

When I heard the title, I almost didn't want to read it. My teacher definitely didn't want me to—at first anyway. She talked about your other books in class, but not that one. So I found out about it from your website. Now I know why my teacher was so weird about it. It's because of what my dad did. He did it, too. He killed my mom. Everyone says I'm not the only one whose dad killed her mom, but I don't know anyone else who it happened to.

My teacher hadn't read the book, so she read it, and then

said I could read it but under one condition—that I agree to see the school counselor before I read it and after I finished it, so I did.

Once I had the book in my hands, I was afraid to start for a few days. Once I did, I didn't want to stop. I cried a lot, but I guess you already knew that. I guess you wanted me to. The book says that Preston is real. I know you say he's real, and the family is real, but is he real-real, or fiction-real?

I have not seen my father since it happened. My aunt and uncle are like Uncle Steve in the book. They hate him and don't ever want me to see him. I don't want to see him either. But sometimes I do. How can you love and hate someone at the same time? That's what you say in the book, and when I read that, I read it again and again, because I know that feeling exactly. The book made me mad, because they forgave him, and we didn't. Why can't I be like Preston? I asked my aunt if I should forgive my dad, and she said I don't have to do anything I don't want to, but I don't know if I don't want to. I feel like Preston—being different from everyone else with this thing that people know about, but don't talk about, and treat you like you'll break if they do talk about it.

Well, thank you for reading my letter. If Preston is real,
I think he's very brave, and I wish he went to my school, be-
cause I'd be his girlfriend, and we could talk about things.
Please write me back, but if you can't, it's okay.

An admirer,
Myra

DEAR MYRA,

Thank you for your letter. Letters like yours remind
me why I write. I'm sorry about what happened in your
family, but I can tell from your letter that you're strong
and have a lot of caring people in your life. I think people aren't really afraid that you'll break when they talk
to you—I think they're afraid that *they'll* break. They're
afraid that they'll say something wrong and never forgive themselves for it. I know that's how I felt when I
first talked to Preston—and, yes, Preston is real-real, not
just fiction-real. I did change his name, though—but
other than that, everything in the story is real.

I don't think anyone can tell you whether or not you should forgive your father. I don't know if I could ever forgive mine if he had killed my mom. Forgiveness is a very difficult thing. That's why I wanted to write the book, because Preston and his family took the hardest path—faith, and the choice to forgive. That choice became their light within the darkness. It's different for everyone though. Don't feel like you have to forgive him, because as Preston found out, pretending to forgive is not the same thing as really forgiving. Whatever you feel, you have a right to feel, and don't let anyone tell you that you have to feel something different.

If there's one thing I learned while writing this book (writers learn things by writing books the same way readers learn things by reading them), it's that forgiveness isn't for the person you're forgiving; forgiveness is for yourself.

I still keep in touch with Preston and his grandmother. I wrote *What Daddy Did* in the early 1990s, when Preston was about fifteen. He's twenty-seven now, became a Special Education teacher, and coached high school track. You might say it's a happy ending, but life—unlike books—keeps going on. In other words, happy endings aren't really endings at all, just high points leading to something else.

Preston had some hard times, too. He lost his temper, got into a fistfight one night, and broke someone's jaw several years ago. He called me and wanted to meet with me because he didn't think anyone else could really understand him. He felt so much of his temper went back directly to what had happened to his mother. He told me he had lost his car in an accident, he was going on trial for the fight and might have to go to jail, and because of that, he lost his job. He felt like his life was over. I gave him some simple wisdom my parents always told me when I thought my world was going to end. They'd say, "This, too, shall pass." No matter how bad things get, they will get better, and then they sometimes get bad again and then sometimes they get great. Well, you get it. During the bad times, keep reminding yourself that there are people around you who care about you a whole lot.

Preston went to trial but didn't go to jail; instead, he did community service. After that, he got another job, got his life back together, and I've heard only good news from him and his grandmother since. I just got a call two weeks ago—his grandmother called to tell me that Preston is getting married next month to a wonderful girl, he loves his job, and has never been happier in his life.

Your life, too, is going to have highs and lows—not because of what you've been through, but because everyone's life does. You've been through a pretty bad low, so when you come to the high points, remember that you deserve to appreciate them. And when the lows come, take a deep breath, dig in, ride them through, and remember that good things must be on the way!

Your friend,

Neal Shusterman

My teacher read Maniac Magee to my class. I'm glad she did. I know a lot about people like Aunt Dot and Uncle Dan who don't talk to each other and even hate each other. They reminded me of my entire neighborhood. My neighborhood is bad. A lot of drug dealers live in my neighborhood, and every day there is a fight and arguments. They do not like to talk stuff out. Instead, they always argue in this neighborhood. I hope all their stuff stops. My brother got shot in the back because of this. Sometimes I want to run away from home like Jeffrey (alias Maniac Magee) did to get away.

Your friend,
Herschel

DEAR HERSCHEL,

I'm glad that you are unhappy about your neighborhood. It means that you know right from wrong, good from bad. I would be more worried about you if you wrote to me: "My neighborhood is good. A lot of people argue and do drugs. It's fun."

So you see, you're on the right track. Don't ever allow yourself to be happy about a bad place. But, don't run away, either.

Easy for me to say, huh? But you're the one living your life, and how are you supposed to make it from day to day? Well, try this:

Look up
Look down
Look in

Okay, what do I mean? Let's take the first: **Look up.** I mean exactly that. How often do you look up? Not much? So do it, even when there's no particular reason to. And I don't mean for five seconds, either. Find a place outside where you can lie down on your back, and look up like you've never looked up before. Feel the sun on your face. Stay long enough to watch a cloud move from one side of the sky to the other.

If there's a safe place at night, do it then, too. Do you have any idea how far away those stars are? It could make you dizzy just to think about it.

So what's the point of all this looking up? The point is to remind yourself that your neighborhood is not all there is. It is not the universe. It is only one puny little scrap of it, and the very same sunlight and moonlight that falls on the drug dealers also falls on really good neighborhoods not far away.

Look down. I don't know where you live, but if it's possible, ask someone to take you to a higher place where you can look down on your neighborhood. The trick is to be far enough away so that you can't see the drug dealers or the arguing people or any bad stuff. Doing this will remind you that the neighborhood is the neighborhood and you are you, and that you can— someday you *will*—walk away from it.

Look in. This is the best one of all. Because guess

what? The street you live on is not your only neighborhood. Know what the other one is? Yourself. Really. You are your own neighborhood—you and your fingers and your runny nose and your dreams and wishes and happys and sads and shivers and tickles and favorite things. You are a neighborhood of one, your own personal zip code. So when the street gets too nasty, isn't it nice to know you can come back inside to yourself?

Do you have family? Do you have friends? Does somebody love you? Do you love somebody? If so— even in the midst of the bad neighborhood—you have the best this world has to offer. The hard times you are going through now will make all the sweeter the good times to come. And they *will* come, Herschel, because time will pass, and you will grow up, and no longer will your neighborhood choose you, but you will choose your neighborhood.

In the meantime, make friends with the clouds and the moon and stars. Make *love* your personal address. Don't let a day go by without saying to someone, "I love you." Are you too shy to say it? No problem. Love is so cool it doesn't even need words. Squeeze a hand. Do a favor. Pick a dandelion and give it away. These are all ways of saying, "I love you."

And say this little verse to yourself every day when you leave the house:

> I am Herschel
> I am good
> I am my own
> Neighborhood

Remember: You will not be living at your present address forever. There are a zillion other addresses and neighborhoods in this wide world, and many of them are good, terrific, even wonderful, and one of them is waiting for you.

Your friend,

Jerry Spinelli

Hi. i am writing to tell you i think you are my favorite writer. My name is lynne, and i am a high school freshman. i was just fumbling around on some sites and found out that you wrote a book on self-injury so i read it. i loved your book Crosses because i could really relate to it. You see, i am fifteen and have been cutting since i was twelve years old. i am big and fat and i used to not have any friends. i used to get pushed and beat all the time by other kids, and i was made fun of because my mom wouldn't allow me to get my ears pierced or wear makeup. A lot of kids have found out about my cutting, as the gossip of small schools travels fast. For the past year I've dealt with the humiliation of other students laughing and mocking me for it. i've tried to stop doing it, but cutting is like a drug for me. It's a true addiction and a bad one at that. You can barely see my arm for the scars. i tried throwing the razor blades away but i either find more or break glasses when i get desperate. i tend to do it when I have a bad argument with someone or if i get depressed *about my weight. My family knows, but they barely ac-knowledge it and do not say anything if they notice recent or fairly recent cuts.*

So, i have some questions that i hope you answer for me. How did you end up writing about self-injury? Was it the fact that so many young people do it today or did you used to do it in the past? Please do not ignore this letter as ig-noring it makes it worse. i can guarantee that i am not some stupid high school kid yanking your chain and want you to know that your help would be a very treasured gift. Please share anything else you have to say about self-injuring for other SIs or people interested in helping a friend or family member with an SI problem. i want you to know your book meant a lot to me.

Your fan,
lynne

P.S. i wish i had my own "Rad the poet" to be my 24/7 friend, but i do have a best friend now. At first, she was shocked but now will do anything to help me. If it weren't for her i would not be alive.

DEAR LYNNE,

Although *Crosses* is a work of fiction, I know what it's like to be a self-injurer. I began cutting myself in high school and continued into college until some close friends intervened. I stopped for several years, and then began again. Finally, I sought professional help. I was diagnosed as bipolar, and a combination of therapy and medication eventually healed me to the point that I no longer cut myself, or even want to . . . so there is hope, and there is help out there.

First of all, you say the adults in your life ignore or don't want to see that you cut yourself. Make them see. If you want help, you have to ask for it—you have to demand it! Contact SAFE Alternatives at 1-800-DONTCUT for advice and information on treatment options in your area. If you Google "self-injury bulletin boards," you will find several places online where self-injurers like yourself post their thoughts, feelings, and advice about cutting. Although your friends want to help you, they don't have the personal experience with your problem to truly understand—young people posting on self-injury bulletin boards can help you because they are going through the same things you are. Also, sharing with them can help you get in touch with yourself.

Of course, you have to want to stop cutting. Maybe you're not ready for that yet—that's okay. Don't beat yourself up with guilt; it will only make things worse. Take healing one step at a time. Don't assume cutting is your biggest problem—it is a symptom. Before you can stop cutting with hope of success, you need to get real with yourself and root out what your real issues are. Maybe you have a chemical imbalance, as I did, or maybe you haven't learned how to deal with adversity in a healthy way. Anxiety and depression are two big reasons for cutting—how can you handle these feelings without cutting? The answers are different for everyone. Get all the help you can, from friends, family, other cutters, therapy . . . but know that in the end, it's *you* who will make the biggest difference in your life.

Cutting, like drugs and alcohol, is a way to escape feelings that seem too hard to handle. You must learn to accept your feelings; they're part of who you are and nothing to be ashamed of. Allow yourself to *feel*, shut your eyes and let the feelings course through you, feel the anger pulsing in your temples and rising up in your throat, feel the sadness twist in your belly and hurt your heart, feel the anxiety making your pulse and thoughts race . . . In my newest book, *Tweaked*, a character says, "The only way through pain is through it." You can't skim over pain and bad feelings with cutting, drugs, or alcohol—not forever—the feelings, unfelt, will stay with you, and grow into something you can't handle safely.

Everyone suffers to some extent from crappy stuff that happens, that they can't help—like being made fun of, or being overweight, or not being pretty enough, smart enough, talented enough, popular enough—whatever. Some problems are bigger than others, and some people, like you, may be more sensitive than others. But you must remember that we all also have an inner strength that can and must be tapped. You have a heart. Use it. Feel with it, believe with it, hope with it.

I wish you all the best in your struggle, and hope I've been some help. Write to me anytime.

Sincerely,

Michelle (Shelley) Stoehr

Shelley Stoehr

I just finished reading Learning to Swim, *and I had to stop what I was doing and write to you right now. I am a seventeen-year-old girl, and I have the same problem as you in your book. I read it and it made me cry. I am afraid to talk about it with my mother, as it is her brother who is doing the abuse. My school counselor says she will talk to me about "anything" but I am afraid.*

This is what I want to know from you personally. Did it take a lot of courage to write that book? How does a person survive such things? How can you talk about them? Does it help to talk?

Please let me know soon. Thank you for reading my letter and I hope you write back. Maybe I'll talk with you.

Yours,
Julianne

DEAR JULIANNE,

Thank you so much for writing. I think it took a lot of courage on your part. And yes, it took courage for me to write *Learning to Swim*. Even now, when I read the poems out loud in public, my heart pounds and my stomach hurts. It is hard to do but important, because your words—my words—can help others talk about what happened to them.

Once, when I read my poems to a college class, a young woman came up afterward with tears in her eyes and said she had been abused, too. She said that reading *Learning to Swim* gave her hope and that she was going to tell her mother about her abuse. We hugged.

I hope you can tell your mother about what happened to you. If, by chance, it is still happening, you must find a trusted adult—if not your mother—who can help. Your guidance counselor sounds like a strong possibility. It will not be easy, and your stomach will probably hurt, but I think—I know—it is the best thing to do. Remember the poem in *LtS* at the end: "Listen. Telling is what matters." That is the truth, as I know it.

It is so painful to bring the words out, but I promise it will help you in the end. It is like puncturing a wound so the pus can run out. Also, your mother (or another adult you trust) needs to know about the abuse so she can prevent it from happening again.

But until you feel brave enough to tell her, please do talk to your school counselor. She may have some good ideas about how to help you.

Please write back. I do care what happens to you, and I know that it is possible to survive abuse and have a good life. The first step is telling the truth; the second step is getting help from a counselor; and the third step is the healing of those hard memories.

Warmly,

Ann Turner

177

Hi. My name is Anne, I'm thirteen, and I just finished reading Hard Love. I loved it, I really did. It was funny at times but deep and meaningful, too. It changed me in many ways. Firstly, it inspired me to keep a diary, where I write all my feelings. Second, it's helped me so much by giving me good things to think about.

Just like anyone, my life isn't picture-perfect. My mom's been kind of depressed lately, and my dad works all the time. It helps me to write letters to them, like Marisol did. I also learned a lot about gay people. I don't think I was ever really prejudiced, but I didn't understand them. I guess I was even scared of them. But now, after knowing Marisol, I know that lesbian and gay people are just regular "normal" people.

I love the sound of Escape Velocity. It's when you're free, totally free. It's like the feeling I get when I'm out on the beach at night and I hear the waves. And I also love the song "Hard Love." It's true that the love that heals our life *is mostly hard love. I love the song. I think I've practically memorized it!*

Anyway, I just wanted to thank you for writing such an excellent book. I hate to admit it, but I got all teary at the end. Well, I'll leave it at this—thank you, Ellen Wittlinger, for teaching me to find myself and inspiring me to start my own 'zine. I'm calling it Dreamscape. *I'm not planning to hand it out or anything like John and Marisol did. It's mainly just for me.*

Thanks again,
Anne

DEAR ANNE,

Thank you so much for writing me such a wonderful letter. I have to admit, your letter made me as tearful as my book made you. I'm so glad that I was the inspiration for you to start writing both a diary and a 'zine. I think writing down your feelings and thoughts is such an important step in getting to know yourself and in helping you come to terms with whatever problems you have in your life.

You're wise to understand that no one's life is "picture-perfect." But, of course, that doesn't make it any easier to deal with your own troubles. I hope your mother is able to find someone to help her with her depression. It sounds like that, combined with your father having to work so much, leaves you rather lonely. As an only child of working parents, I was often lonely growing up, too—reading and writing kept me company when people couldn't. You've obviously learned that lesson, too.

I think the thing that makes me happiest about your letter is your admission that though you were once scared of homosexuality, now, "after knowing Marisol," you see that they are "regular 'normal' people." The fact that Marisol was so real to you that you felt you knew her is thrilling to me. You've given me a terrific gift by letting me know that my character has changed, in such a positive way, how you view the world.

I hope you enjoy writing *Dreamscape.* Thank you so much for the inspiration you've given *me*—now I know there are readers out there who are reading my books in the way every author hopes—with their whole hearts. Maybe someday you'll know what that feels like. For now, I hope you feel good knowing that I read and responded to your letter with my whole heart.

Yours sincerely,

Ellen Wittlinger

ABOUT LAURIE HALSE ANDERSON

Laurie Halse Anderson has loved to write since she was a little girl. She attributes her start to her second-grade teacher, who started her writing haiku. Although she doesn't write much poetry, Laurie loves studying different cultures and even went so far as to work on a pig farm in Denmark as an exchange student. Before she decided that she wanted a career as an author, Laurie spent time as a reporter and a stockbroker, cleaned banks, and even milked cows. In addition to young adult novels, Laurie also writes picture books and chapter books for young children and enjoys traveling around the country speaking at schools and conferences. Laurie has four loves: her family (husband, three daughters, and a son), her writing career, where she lives (Mexico, NY, where there's abundant snow), and when people pronounce her full name correctly (it's Halse, like "waltz").

If you'd like to read more books by Laurie Halse Anderson, here are some suggestions:

Catalyst (New York: Viking, 2004), 240 pp.

Overachiever Kate Malone, devastated when she learns she wasn't accepted at MIT, thinks her world will crumble until a tragedy at her neighbors' house puts things into perspective.

Prom (New York: Viking, 2005), 224 pp.

Unlike her classmates, senior Ashley Hannigan couldn't care less about the prom—until a teacher sponsor runs away with all the money less than two weeks before the event.

Speak (New York: Farrar, Straus and Giroux, 1999), 208 pp.

After she calls the police to a summer party, Melinda Sordino's friends abandon her and her peers harass her. Melinda is physically unable to speak about the terrible events of that night until her art class and a caring teacher help her find her voice.

To learn more about Laurie Halse Anderson and her books, visit this website: **www.writerlady.com**

ABOUT SANDY ASHER

Sandy Asher practically grew up in her neighborhood public library in Philadelphia, so it is no wonder that she's spent most of her life writing novels, stories, plays, and poems for young adults and children. She has written more than two dozen books and as many plays. In addition to traveling all over the country speaking at schools and conferences, she has directed a children's theater company and other projects at Drury University; is a member of The Dramatists Guild; and is co-founder of the website USA Plays for Kids. Her plays are published by Anchorage Press (www.applays.com) and Dramatic Publishing Company (www. dramaticpublishing.com). Sandy currently lives in Pennsylvania with her husband, Harvey, two cats, and a dog.

If you'd like to read more books by Sandy Asher or explore her works for the stage, here are some suggestions:

▶ *Dancing with Strangers* (Woodstock, IL: Dramatic Publishing, 1995, 1993), D59
Adapted from her novel *Out of Here: A Senior Class Yearbook* (New York: Puffin, 1995), 160 pp.

In this collection of three one-act plays, the characters explore the roles human relationships play in life: divorce, pregnancy, loneliness, and the beginnings and breakups of romances are among topics addressed.

Everything Is Not Enough (Woodstock, IL: Dramatic Publishing, 1987), E50.

Adapted from her novel of the same name (New York: Random House, 1987), 168 pp.

Michael struggles to tell his father that he wants to become a social worker rather than go into the family jewelry business. The two are in conflict until Michael's father realizes that Michael needs to leave his protective shell and explore the outside world.

I Will Sing Life: Voices from the Hole in the Wall Gang Camp (Woodstock, IL: Dramatic Publishing, 2000), I67.

Adapted from a nonfiction book of the same name by Larry Berger, Dahlia Lithwick, and Seven Campers (New York: Little, Brown, & Co., 1992), 206 pp.

This play is based on the writings of and interviews with young people attending the Hole in the Wall Gang Camp, founded by actor Paul Newman for children with life-threatening illnesses.

To learn more about Sandy Asher and her books and plays, visit this website: **usaplays4kids.drury.edu/playwrights/asher**

ABOUT T. A. BARRON

T. A. Barron lives in Colorado with his wife, Currie, and their five children. He enjoys writing, hiking, and spending time with his family, especially outdoors. Besides writing, Mr. Barron is heavily involved in environmental issues. He created the Gloria Barron Prize for Young Heroes Award (www.barronprize.org), a national award in honor of his mother's work to help the deaf and blind experience nature. The annual prizes honor teens who have done outstanding work on behalf of the environment and for humanity. Mr. Barron believes that everyone has a hero inside and that everyone can make this world a better place to live.

If you'd like to read more books by T. A. Barron, here are some suggestions:

The Ancient One (New York: Philomel Books, 1992), 368 pp.
     To find the secret of a lost Native American tribe, Kate travels back in time through an ancient tree that is also a time tunnel.

The Hero's Trail: A Hiking Guide for a Heroic Life (New York: Philomel Books, 2002), 160 pp.
     Exemplifying his belief that anyone can be a hero, Barron's book is full of true, inspiring stories about the heroic feats of young people from all backgrounds.

The Lost Years of Merlin, Book I (New York: Philomel Books, 1996), 284 pp.
     When a young boy with no memory of his past washes up on a mysterious island, he sets out to discover his identity, unaware that he is actually a great wizard. (Five books in this epic.)

To learn more about T. A. Barron and his books, visit this website:
www.tabarron.com

ABOUT JOAN BAUER

Joan Bauer lives in Brooklyn with her husband, Evan, and daughter, Jean. This *New York Times* best-selling author began her career in writing after she successfully worked in advertising sales. Joan wrote her first young adult novel, *Squashed*, while recuperating from severe neck and back injuries sustained in a car accident. Being able to laugh while writing the book pulled her through the tough times. Incorporating humor into the difficulties of life remains one of her goals in writing.

If you'd like to read more books by Joan Bauer, here are some suggestions:

Backwater (New York: G. P. Putnam's Sons, 2000, c. 1999), 224 pp.

A misfit in a family where everyone is expected to become a lawyer, history lover Ivy Breedlove sets out to find her reclusive aunt Jo. In Aunt Jo, Ivy finds a kindred spirit who helps her better understand both family expectations and family ties.

Hope Was Here (New York: G. P. Putnam's Sons, 2002, c. 2000), 192 pp.

Hope is skeptical when she and her aunt Addie first arrive in a tiny midwestern dairy town, but this small town has a big heart. Will she finally realize her dream of putting down roots in a place where people care about her?

Rules of the Road (New York: G. P. Putnam's Sons, 1999, c. 1998), 208 pp.

Jenna Boller, a top-notch shoe salesperson, is delighted to escape her difficult life when her boss, Mrs. Gladstone, hires Jenna to drive her to Texas. During the trip, Jenna learns about shoes, responsibility, truth, and how to love her dad—even if he is an alcoholic. Readers can learn more about Jenna in the companion book, *Best Foot Forward* (G. P. Putnam's Sons, 2005).

To learn more about Joan Bauer and her books, visit this website:
www.joanbauer.com

ABOUT MARION DANE BAUER

A former English teacher, Marion Dane Bauer is the author of more than fifty children's books, young adult books, and effective writing handbooks. Her first work was a poem in tribute to her beloved teddy bear. Since then, writing has served many times as the outlet for her passions. She is currently on the faculty of Vermont College's MFA in Writing for Children and Young Adults. Marion lives in Minnesota with her partner of nineteen years and enjoys biking, camping, and walking outdoors with her grandchildren.

If you'd like to read more books by Marion Dane Bauer, here are some suggestions:

Face to Face (New York: Clarion, 1991), 176 pp.

Michael, a troubled teen who idolizes the father who deserted him and resents his stepfather, must finally face the truth about his real father. Disillusioned, humiliated, and furious, Michael comes close to committing suicide.

On My Honor (New York: Clarion, 1986), 96 pp.

Joel swears to his father that he and Tony will only go to the park, but Tony persuades him to race to the sandbar in the river. When Tony never makes it to the sandbar, a guilt-ridden Joel must deal with the consequences.

Runt (New York: Clarion, 2002), 138 pp.

Runt is the last born and smallest of a litter of wolf cubs. Told from Runt's perspective, the story details his attempts to keep up with his bigger and stronger littermates, and his inability to gain acceptance from his father, King.

To learn more about Marion Dane Bauer and her books, visit this website:
www.mariondanebauer.com

ABOUT CHERIE BENNETT

With an educator/actress for a mother and a television writer (*The Twilight Zone* and *Route 66*) for a father, Cherie Bennett grew up in a Detroit show business family. Though she always loved to write, she attended the University of Michigan as a musical theater major, then went to New York City and became a Broadway actress and a singer. It was her experience in the theater that led her back to the page—not as a novelist, but as a playwright for adults. Cherie and her husband and frequent coauthor, Jeff Gottesfeld, currently live in Salt Lake City, Utah, with their son Igor and a friendly cat named Bubba. Cherie enjoys travel, theater, film, reading, and cooking, and is an ace Boggle player. Known as the author who writes back, she has answered more than 15,000 letters and e-mails (authorchik@aol.com) in recent years. Those letters spawned her widely syndicated teen advice column, "Hey, Cherie!," for the *San Diego Union Tribune* and Copley News Service.

If you'd like to read more books by Cherie Bennett or explore her works for the stage, here are some suggestions:

With Jeff Gottesfeld, *Anne Frank and Me* (New York: G. P. Putnam's Sons, 2001), 352 pp.

Nicole Burns doubts that the Holocaust or Anne Frank's diary have any relevance to her own life until she travels back to 1942, where she is a privileged Jewish girl in Nazi-occupied France. Captured by the Nazis, Nicole meets the real Anne Frank on the way to Auschwitz and discovers that she and Anne are more alike than she realized.

With Jeff Gottesfeld, *A Heart Divided* (New York: Delacorte, 2004), 320 pp.

With the help of local boy Jack, Kate has just begun to appreciate the culture of her new home in the South. A petition to replace the Confederate flag as the school symbol engenders a bitter controversy.

Life in the Fat Lane (New York: Laurel Leaf, 1999, c. 1998), 260 pp.

Prom Queen Lara Ardeche has the perfect life until she inexplicably gains 100 pounds and is diagnosed with the rare (and fictitious) metabolic disorder "Axwell-Crowne Syndrome."

To learn more about Cherie Bennett and her books, visit this website:
www.cheriebennett.com

ABOUT EDWARD BLOOR

Edward Bloor grew up writing stories to entertain himself, his friends, and his family in Trenton, New Jersey. He later became a middle-school language arts teacher in Fort Lauderdale, Florida. Currently, he edits educational materials for Harcourt School Publishers, writes books, and speaks to teachers and students all over the country about his own award-winning novels. He lives in Winter Garden, Florida, with his wife, Pam, a teacher, and their two children, Amanda and Spencer.

If you'd like to read more books by Edward Bloor, here are some suggestions:

Crusader (New York: Harcourt, 1997), 400 pp.

Quiet Roberta works in a mall arcade full of games that promote violence and disrespect for minorities. Terrible events at the mall force Roberta to face her own mother's brutal murder and give her the courage to speak out in a crusade against violence.

London Calling (New York: Alfred A. Knopf, 2006), 304 pp.

Martin experiences a summer he'll never forget, one that involves a boy asking for his help during World War II; the problem is that Martin lives in the twenty-first century.

Story Time (New York: Harcourt, 2004), 424 pp.

The Whittaker Magnet School is supposed to be a great institution, but George and Kate find out it's not all it's cracked up to be. It may feature high standardized test scores, but what about that murderous demon in the library?

To learn more about Edward Bloor and his books, visit this website:
www.edwardbloor.net

ABOUT SUE ELLEN BRIDGERS

Sue Ellen Bridgers attributes her love for stories to both of her grand-mothers and her strength and determination to her mother. Her south-ern background inspires her writings—her characters speak in a southern dialect and typically have traditional southern names, and her settings reflect southern towns. Sue Ellen travels the country, speaking about her writing while stressing the options and opportunities available to young people, especially young women. She currently lives in North Carolina with Ben, her husband of nearly forty years, and is working on a new book about two boys in love with the same girl.

If you'd like to read more books by Sue Ellen Bridgers, here are some sug-gestions:

▶ *All Together Now* (Wilmington, NC: Banks Channel Books, 2001, c. 1976), 244 pp.

Twelve-year-old Casey pretends to be a boy around her new thirty-three-year-old, mentally disabled friend Dwayne because she fears he won't want to play sports with a girl. When Dwayne learns the truth, his reaction is more honest than others'.

▶ *All We Know of Heaven* (Wilmington, NC: Banks Channel Books, 1999, c. 1996), 204 pp.

Bethany, whose mother died and whose father is a neglectful alco-holic, has yearned for real love all her life. When she meets and marries Joel, she thinks she's found love at last—until Joel's violent temper has tragic consequences.

▶ *Permanent Connections* (Wilmington, NC: Banks Channel Books, 1999, c. 1987), 264 pp.

Rob, a city boy, is sent to rural North Carolina after having trouble with alcohol and drugs, and connects with Ellery, another city kid. Facing important choices teaches both boys about consequences and the value of permanent connections.

To learn more about Sue Ellen Bridgers and her books, visit this website:
www.sueellenbridgers.com

ABOUT CHRIS CRUTCHER

In addition to writing numerous novels, including several award winners, Chris Crutcher worked as an educator for approximately twelve years. He was also a child-family therapist specializing in child abuse for more than twenty years. His gifts of empathy with and understanding of other people enable him to portray emotions powerfully in his stories. Chris bases his novels somewhat on his own experiences and tries to depict life with honesty and humor. He currently lives in Spokane, Washington, and speaks at schools and conferences all over the United States. His most recent claim to fame is that every one of his nine young adult novels appears on banned book lists.

If you'd like to read more books by Chris Crutcher, here are some suggestions:

Chinese Handcuffs (New York: Greenwillow, 1991), 220 pp.
Dillon Hemingway is dealing with the double trauma of being abandoned by his mother and watching his older brother Preston commit suicide. Helping Jennifer Lawless, a sexual abuse victim, gives Dillon some closure.

▶ *Ironman* (New York: Greenwillow, 1995), 228 pp.

Bo Brewster's violent outbursts at school land him in anger management class, where he develops the trust he needs to admit that his anger and self-hatred arise from feeling helpless against his father's abuse.

▶ *Staying Fat for Sarah Byrnes* (New York: Greenwillow, 1993), 216 pp.

Best friends Eric "Moby" Calhoun, who is fat, and Sarah Byrnes, who is severely scarred and disfigured, always support each other. But can even Moby reach Sarah to find out what has made her go catatonic?

To learn more about Chris Crutcher and his books, visit this website:
www.aboutcrutcher.com

ABOUT CHRISTOPHER PAUL CURTIS

From factory worker to award-winning novelist, Christopher Paul Curtis credits his becoming a writer to two reasons: his love of words and his love for his wife. During the thirteen years he spent hanging car doors on large Buicks at the historically famous Fisher Body Plant #1, he used to spend his breaks getting away from the assembly line by writing. Prodded by his wife, he took a year off and wrote his first novel, *The Watsons Go to Birmingham—1963*, while sitting in a public library. Shortly after its publication and immediate success, Christopher moved from Flint, Michigan, to Ontario, Canada, where he currently lives with his wife, Kay, and their two children, Cydney and Steven.

If you'd like to read more books by Christopher Paul Curtis, here are some suggestions:

Bucking the Sarge (New York: Wendy Lamb Books, 2004), 272 pp.

Luther's mother, aka "the Sarge," is a slumlord who's trying to make money at the expense of her values and everyone else's. Will Luther make it out of Flint and into college, or will his mother have her way and get him to take over the family business?

Bud, Not Buddy (New York: Delacorte, 1999), 256 pp.

Set during the Depression, ten-year-old Bud runs away from an awful foster home in search of the man he believes is his biological father.

The Watsons Go to Birmingham—1963 (New York: Delacorte, 1995), 224 pp.

Readers will be riveted by the story of one family's vacation during the Civil Rights movement. Based on an actual trip Christopher took with his family to Florida, the story took a shift when his son, Steven, brought home a poem by Dudley Randall, "Ballad of Birmingham," that tells about the racially motivated bombing of a black church.

To learn more about Christopher Paul Curtis and his books, visit this website: **www.randomhouse.com/features/christopherpaulcurtis**

ABOUT LOIS DUNCAN

Lois Duncan has been writing since the age of ten, and it's as though being a writer was her destiny. She was greatly influenced by her very talented and internationally renowned parents, Joseph and Lois Steinmetz, who were magazine photographers. She taught for several years in the Journalism Department at the University of New Mexico and wrote hundreds of articles and short stories for various magazines. She has also written approximately fifty books and is probably best known as a mystery and suspense novelist. In 1997, two of her novels were made into films: *I Know What You Did Last Summer*, starring Jennifer Love Hewitt and Sarah Michelle Gellar, and *Killing Mr. Griffin*, starring Scott Bairstow and Amy Jo Johnson. Lois Duncan currently lives in Sarasota, Florida, with her husband and best friend, Don Arquette.

If you'd like to read more books by Lois Duncan, here are some suggestions:

▶ *I Know What You Did Last Summer* (New York: Little, Brown, 1993), 208 pp.

One night, four teenagers' lives are changed forever when their car strikes a boy and they leave the scene of the accident without even checking on his condition. They swear one another to secrecy after learning of his death, but a year later someone sends them each a newspaper clipping of the accident with a note saying, "I know what you did last summer."

▶ *Killing Mr. Griffin* (New York: Bantam Doubleday Dell, 1978), 223 pp.

Five high school students plan a prank to get even with Mr. Griffin, their strict English teacher. Unbeknownst to them, Mr. Griffin has a heart condition and things go from bad to beyond worse, as these teenagers have to figure out what to do after his fatal heart attack.

▶ *Who Killed My Daughter?* (New York: Laurel Leaf, 1994, c. 1992), 368 pp.

Duncan's daughter Kaitlyn was murdered in New Mexico in 1989, and this book is the author's attempt to make sense of the insensible. The crime remains unsolved to this day.

To learn more about Lois Duncan and her books, visit this website:
http://loisduncan.arquettes.com/Biography3.htm

ABOUT ALEX FLINN

Although Alexandra "Alex" Flinn became a lawyer after college, she later had a bigger pull to be a writer instead. Perhaps it was her mother's suggestion that she become a writer when Alex was five years old and writing poetry. Perhaps it was because she always chose to read literature instead of doing the "programmed readers" required in elementary school. Perhaps it was her moving and "not fitting in" during middle school that propelled Alex to read and write to pass that painful time. Whatever the reason, her choosing to read and write helped her make friends in high school and also gain acceptance in a performing arts program for the gifted and talented. Law school introduced her to women who had been beaten by their boyfriends or husbands; she also learned that more than a fourth of teenage girls have been hit by their boyfriends. *Breathing Underwater*, published in 2001 and an ALA Top-10 Best Book for Young Adults, was the culmination of her passion for and experience with this issue. Since then, Alex Flinn has written three more award-winning books with a fifth one—*Diva* (a companion to *Breathing Underwater*)—coming soon. Alex Flinn currently lives with her husband, two daughters, a dog and a cat in Miami, Florida.

If you'd like to read more books by Alex Flinn, here are some suggestions:

▶ *Breathing Underwater* (New York: HarperCollins, 2001), 263 pp.

Nick may be popular at school, but his abusive father regards him as a "loser" at home. When things don't go exactly right with his girlfriend, Nick strikes out in more than one way.

▶ *Fade to Black* (New York: HarperTempest, 2005),184 pp.

Three students' lives become intertwined and tangled when Alex, who is HIV positive, is attacked by one and his attacker is accused by another. Who's right? Who's wrong? Who knows in this mystery drama?

Nothing to Lose (New York: HarperTempest, 2004), 288 pp.

In this mystery, Michael, whose alias, Robert Frost, has helped him hide as a runaway at a carnival, has to decide whether to keep hiding or to help his mother, who's been charged with murder.

To learn more about Alex Flinn and her books, visit this website:
www.alexflinn.com

ABOUT ADRIAN FOGELIN

For Adrian Fogelin, good things come in threes. When she was little, she always wanted a dog, a canopy bed, and a diary. It was the diary that got her writing off to a good start, though she also credits her mother, a writer herself, who had a profound influence on Adrian's ability to tell stories. Adrian began her career, however, as an artist (while living on a boat, having a baby, and starting a business), had a second career as a librarian of sorts (shelving books, checking out books, issuing library cards), and finally settled into her third career as a writer (and a consultant, mother, and wife). Now her life is blessed by her three loves: her family, her career, and Florida.

If you'd like to read more books by Adrian Fogelin, here are some suggestions:

The Big Nothing (Atlanta, GA: Peachtree Publishers, 2004), 235 pp.

At thirteen, Justin has learned that by zoning out and going to "the big nothing," he can escape the pain in his life. A newly discovered talent for music helps him makes sense of his troubles.

Crossing Jordan (Atlanta, GA: Peachtree Publishers, 2000), 160 pp.

Cassie and Jemmie don't see each other as just "white" and "black," but their parents do. Cassie describes how her friend and neighbor becomes her running and reading partner and manages to change both families' viewpoints about each other.

Sister Spider Knows All (Atlanta, GA: Peachtree Publishers, 2003), 209 pp.

Roxanne is being raised by her loving grandmother Mimi, but where is Roxanne's mom, and why won't Mimi talk about her? When Rox finds her mother's old diary, she begins a quest to find her true family.

To learn more about Adrian Fogelin and her books, visit this website:
www.adrianfogelin.com

ABOUT NANCY GARDEN

Nancy Garden is an award-winning novelist who tackles the issue of homophobia with clarity and insight. No matter what age or sexuality, her readers find that they can either relate to the characters' feelings or understand them in a different way. Nancy attributes her love for writing and books to her mother's family, and she enjoys writing in several genres: fantasy, contemporary and historical fiction, and picture books. She resides in New England with her partner of more than thirty years.

If you'd like to read more books by Nancy Garden, here are some suggestions:

▶ *Annie on My Mind* (New York: Farrar, Straus & Giroux, 1992, c. 1982), 234 pp.

This novel is among the first books to show two lesbians, Liza and Annie, learning to accept their love for each other. Their story isn't without struggle, but their love survives.

▶ *Endgame* (New York: Harcourt, 2006), 304 pp.

A fourteen-year-old boy is the victim of all kinds of bullying. The question is, how long can Gray last before his pent-up frustration and anger get the better of him?

▶ *Good Moon Rising* (New York: Farrar, Straus & Giroux, 1996), 240 pp.

Jan unexpectedly loses the main role of Elizabeth Procter in *The Crucible* to Kerry, and the drama teacher appoints Jan as the stage manager instead. While Jan trains Kerry for her part, the two fall in love, initiating a slew of accusations from other cast members. (Note: This is out of print in the original edition, but may be ordered in a print-on-demand edition from iUniverse at www.iUniverse.com or by calling 1-800-288-4677.)

To learn more about Nancy Garden and her books, visit this website:
www.nancygarden.com

ABOUT PATRICIA HERMES

Patricia Hermes is the author of many books for young people, from early grades through young adult. She focuses on subjects that kids care about, and because of that, some of her books are filled with sadness— but many others are filled with the joy and playfulness of children. When not involved with her writing, teaching, and lecturing, Patricia enjoys running, playing the piano, reading, and visiting with friends and her beloved children and grandchildren, many of whom serve as the inspiration for her novels.

If you'd like to read more books by Patricia Hermes, here are some suggestions:

Cheat the Moon (Boston: Little, Brown, 1998), 167 pp.

After her mother's death, Gabby is forced to care for the household as well as provide care for her little brother, Will. Gabby's father is well meaning, but his alcoholism interferes with their lives. A tragedy brings Gabby's great-grandma to help Gabby love and trust again.

Summer Secrets (Tarrytown, NY: Marshall Cavendish, 2004), 141 pp.

Set during a long, hot summer in Mississippi during the 1940s, this book introduces readers to a middle school girl's thoughts about racism and her mother's mental illness via her journal entries.

Sweet By and By (New York: HarperCollins, 2002), 192 pp.

Through music and the wonder of living in the mountains of Tennessee, Blessing—who's been raised by her grandmother after losing her grandfather and both parents when she was a baby—must elicit courage and faith to survive when her grandmother's health fails.

To learn more about Patricia Hermes and her books, visit this website:
www.authorsillustrators.com/hermes/hermes.htm

ABOUT SARA HOLBROOK

Performance poet Sara Holbrook grew up the older of two sisters in Berkley, Michigan, a suburb just outside Detroit. The first time she ever saw anyone "perform" a poem was her seventh-grade English class, when the teacher, Mrs. Housch, galloped around the room while she read "The Midnight Ride of Paul Revere." After graduating from high school, Sara moved to Alliance, Ohio, where she earned a bachelor's degree in English from Mount Union College. When her two daughters, Katie and Kelly, were little, she did some substitute teaching but then got into public relations, writing newsletters, press releases, speeches, and brochures. She made a dream come true for herself when she became a full-time poet in 1993. Sara Holbrook enjoys walking, cooking, reading, and playing with her Boston terrier. She currently lives in Mentor, Ohio, and travels the country performing her poetry and teaching writing, using her books *WHAM! It's a Poetry Jam* (Boyds Mills Press, 2002) and *Practical Poetry: A Nonstandard Approach to Meeting Content-Area Standards* (Heinemann, 2005).

If you'd like to read more books by Sara Holbrook, here are some suggestions:

▶ *By Definition: Poems of Feelings,* illustrated by Scott Mattern (Honesdale, PA: Boyds Mills Press, 2003), 48 pp.

High school is tough when hormones are flying and emotions are, too. These poems address love and lies, disappointment and doubt, truth and trust among other questions and issues that arise during this volatile period in one's development.

▶ *I Never Said I Wasn't Difficult* (Honesdale, PA: Boyds Mills Press, 1997), 48 pp.

Teenagers across America will find a poem in this collection that they will swear was written specifically for them. The poems focus on relationships and subsequent emotions relating to family, friends, and school.

▶ *Walking on the Boundaries of Change* (Honesdale, PA: Boyds Mills Press, 1998), 64 pp.

This collection of poems targets middle school and somewhat older teens who face challenges, changes, and choices as they mature. Issues of sexuality and gangs, respect and truth, hope and friendship are among the many topics addressed.

To learn more about Sara Holbrook and her books of poems, visit this website: **www.saraholbrook.com**

ABOUT CATHERINE RYAN HYDE

Catherine Ryan Hyde is a full-time, award-winning writer of mostly adult novels and short stories. One of her best-known young adult novels, *Pay It Forward*, was released by Warner Brothers as a motion picture starring Academy Award winners Kevin Spacey and Helen Hunt, and Academy Award nominee Haley Joel Osment. Two of her other adult novels, *Electric God* (Simon & Schuster, 2000) and *Walter's Purple Heart* (Simon & Schuster, 2002), have been selected for the big screen as well. Catherine Ryan Hyde currently lives with her beloved dog in Cambria, California, where she also teaches fiction workshops at the Cuesta College Writers' Conference. Her next young adult book, *The Year of My Miraculous Reappearance* (Knopf, 2007), is about a thirteen-year-old who doesn't want to become like her alcoholic, broken mother.

If you'd like to read more books by Catherine Ryan Hyde, here are some suggestions:

Becoming Chloe (New York: Alfred A. Knopf, 2006), 224 pp.

Jordy runs away from his disapproving parents and meets up with Chloe, another runaway who's suffered an unusual number of bad events but still has a survival spirit about her.

Love in the Present Tense (New York: Doubleday, 2006), 272 pp.

Pearl's life changes forever when she gets pregnant and shoots the father of her baby on her thirteenth birthday.

Pay It Forward (New York: Pocket Books, 2000), 320 pp.

Margaret Meade is known for her famous statement, "Never doubt that a small group of committed citizens can change the world. Indeed, it's the only thing that has." Trevor McKinney shows us how *one person* can make a positive difference in the world by the "pay it forward" concept.

To learn more about Catherine Ryan Hyde and her books, visit this website: **www.cryanhyde.com**

ABOUT JOAN F. KAYWELL

Joan F. Kaywell is a full professor of English Education at the University of South Florida, where she has won several teaching awards. She is passionate about assisting preservice and practicing teachers in discovering ways to improve literacy and believes that books save lives; she's living proof! It is her hope that those who read this book will find an author who "speaks" to them and then read the books listed. Dr. Kaywell advocates reading as a healthful escape from life's challenges and often says, "There's hope in a book!"

She donates her time extensively to the National Council of Teachers of English (NCTE) and its Florida affiliate (FCTE): she is past president of NCTE's Assembly on Literature for Adolescents (ALAN) and is currently serving as its membership secretary. A portion of the royalties of this book will be donated to ALAN, a special interest group devoted to showcasing the use of young adult literature in the classroom. Please visit www.alan-ya.org for more information about this dynamic group of teachers, authors, librarians, publishers, teacher educators, and students.

Dr. Kaywell is published in several journals and regularly reviews young adult novels for *The ALAN Review*. She has edited two series of textbooks: four volumes of *Adolescent Literature as a Complement to the Classic* (1993, 1995, 1997, 2000); and six volumes of *Using Literature to Help Troubled Teenagers Cope with [Various] Issues* (Family 1999, Societal [Carroll] 1999, Identity [Kaplan] 1999, Health [Bowman] 2000, End-of-Life [Allen] 2000, Abuse 2004); and has written one: *Adolescents At Risk: A Guide to Fiction and Nonfiction for Young Adults, Parents, and Professionals* (1993). This work, *Dear Author: Letters of Hope*, is her first trade book.

To learn more about Joan F. Kaywell and her work, visit this website:
www.coedu.usf.edu/kaywell

ABOUT ANNE C. LEMIEUX

After graduating from Simmons College in Boston, where she majored in writing and minored in illustration, Anne took time to marry, have children, study music, and live life. Now A. C. LeMieux enjoys writing for a variety of audiences. In order to make her characters more believable, Anne researches them before beginning her book. Her female characters are strong and independent, which makes a lot of sense considering Anne grew up with six brothers and no sisters. Her image of women goes outside the usual feminine roles, and it's important to her to pass that on to her readers. For example, her latest work, *LoveSpeed* (Atheneum, 2007), features a senior girl's struggle with choices for her future and being her special-needs' brother's keeper. Currently, Anne LeMieux lives in Connecticut with her husband and son and has a daughter in college.

If you'd like to read more books by Anne C. LeMieux, here are some suggestions:

Dare to Be, M.E.! (New York: William Morrow, 1998, c. 1997), 240 pp.

Justine and Mary Ellen are both academically talented, but these best friends take two completely different paths when Justine goes away to Paris. In one summer, Justine becomes boy-crazy and develops an eating disorder, whereas Mary Ellen sees more value in being herself.

Do Angels Sing the Blues? (New York: Avon Flare, 1996, c. 1995), 215 pp.

Boog and Theo are best friends who play in a blues band. This story is about music and the death of a best friend, seeds sown in the author's personal experience.

The T.V. Guidance Counselor (New York: William Morrow, 1993), 240 pp.

Unable to cope with his parents' divorce, Michael gets depressed and withdraws behind the lens of his camera, from where he can safely view the world. Janey, a strange woman who repeatedly picks up and becomes absorbed by a *TV Guide*, intrigues Michael and she becomes his focus.

To learn more about Anne C. LeMieux and her books, visit this website:
**www.harpercollinschildrens.com/HarperChildrens/Teachers/
Authorsandillustrators/contributordetail.aspx?CId=17398**

ABOUT CHRIS LYNCH

Chris Lynch has been writing since 1993 and figures that if he hadn't become a writer, he would have become a mess instead. His two favorite books are *Fox in Sox* by Dr. Seuss and *The Chocolate War* by Robert Cormier—the former for its rhythm and fun, and the latter because of the intense emotional response it evoked in him. Chris's writing tends to have characters who do more damage to themselves than to others, and sports tend to be a central focus as a better way to expend energy than violence. He gets his ideas from fragments of his memories and whatever catches his attention. Chris Lynch alternates between living in Boston and in Scotland and enjoys being with his children and walking Chunk, his springer spaniel.

If you'd like to read more books by Chris Lynch, here are some suggestions:

Inexcusable (New York: Athenaeum, 2005), 176 pp.

A likable senior football player known as Killer Keir defends his honor after being accused of raping the girl he loves. From the first line— "The way it looks is not the way it is"—to the last, readers will see how two people can see the same event in totally different ways.

▶ *Slot Machine* (New York: HarperTrophy, 1996), 256 pp.

Fourteen-year-old Elvin Bishop can be described by three F's: he's friendly, he's funny, and he's fat. Imagine what attending an all-boys Catholic high school orientation camp will be like for him, an unathletic guy trying to find the "slot" that is right for him.

▶ *Who the Man* (New York: HarperCollins, 2002), 192 pp.

Earl Pryor is big and he's bad—or so everyone says and thinks about him. When this thirteen-year-old gets suspended for fighting, the unwelcomed time off from school makes him confront his family (which is falling apart), his views on religion, and his feelings for an older girl.

To learn more about Chris Lynch and his books, visit this website:
**www.harpercollinschildrens.com/HarperChildrens/Kids/Authors
AndIllustrators/ContributorDetail.aspx?Cld=12419**

ABOUT JANET MCDONALD

Janet McDonald was nearly born inside a taxicab in New York. She was then raised by her parents in public housing in Brooklyn with four brothers and two sisters. Her first escape from the Farragut Housing Projects was simply reading books. This escape served her well as she eventually earned three degrees: French literature from Vassar College, law from New York University, and journalism from Columbia University. Janet McDonald's life is a testimonial to persistence and strength and of a woman's real struggle to achieve her parents' wish for her—to get out of the 'hood. Currently, she lives in Paris, France, where she practices law, writes books, and tours the world promoting reading, education, and justice.

If you'd like to read more books by Janet McDonald, here are some suggestions:

▶ *Harlem Hustle* (New York: Farrar, Straus & Giroux, 2006), 192 pp.
    After Eric's drug-abusing parents drop him off to fend for himself in the city streets, Eric must fight the odds and various temptations to pursue his dream of becoming a famous rapper.

▶ *Project Girl* (New York: Farrar, Straus & Giroux, 2000, c. 1999), 233 pp.
    In this memoir, readers see how the human spirit can overcome poverty. (Note: Janet's younger brother and best friend, Kevin McDonald, published a book of his own—*Project Boy*—in 2004.)

▶ *Spellbound* (New York: Farrar, Straus & Giroux, 2004), 144 pp.
    Raven never thought that she would be a sixteen-year-old mother like her unmotivated best friend Aisha (from *Chill Wind*). Unlike Aisha, who's content sitting around all day watching TV and hanging out, Raven wants more for herself and proves that a strong will can beat the odds.

To learn more about Janet McDonald and her books, visit this website:
www.projectgirl.com

ABOUT RODMAN PHILBRICK

Rodman Philbrick grew up in New Hampshire, where he fell in love with writing (not the rejection letters) and the seacoast. Determined to be a writer, he allowed nothing to stand in his way and worked a number of odd jobs to keep his life afloat: he's been a longshoreman, a boatbuilder, and a storyteller. A screenwriter and an award-winning novelist, Philbrick is best known for *Freak the Mighty*, which was made into a feature film. Rodman Philbrick married editor and writer Lynn Harnett, and they alternate between living in the Florida Keys and in Maine, depending on the time of year. When he's not writing, you can bet he's fishing. Let it be known that in the Philbrick household it's only "catch and release"—unless fish is on the menu!

If you'd like to read more books by Rodman Philbrick, here are some suggestions:

▶ *Freak the Mighty* (New York: Scholastic, 1993), 173 pp.

Two teenagers who are continuously tormented by their peers due to their disabilities become friends. Together, using their strengths—Max's size and Kevin's mind—they form a team that fights against badness.

▶ *Last Book in the Universe* (New York: Scholastic, 2000), 223 pp.

Set in a dreary futuristic society where mind probes are used to wipe out memories, this book focuses on Spaz, whose exceptionality prevents him from losing his memory. He learns why it's essential that the past be remembered and begins a quest to change the societal practice.

▶ *The Young Man and the Sea* (New York: Scholastic, 2005), 192 pp.

After his mother's death, twelve-year-old Samuel "Skiff" Beaman decides to do something proactive to earn money rather than follow in his father's beer-drinking depression—he single-handedly takes a small wooden boat out to sea to catch a big tuna.

To learn more about Rodman Philbrick, his books and movie, visit this website:
www.rodmanphilbrick.com

ABOUT MARILYN REYNOLDS

Drawing on decades of experience working with at-risk students in an alternative high school in California, Reynolds's realistic teen fiction takes on tough issues that permeate the lives of many of today's teens: abuse, pregnancy, rape, racism, gay/lesbian harassment, and a myriad of other subissues. In addition to her eight books of teen fiction, one for which Reynolds received an Emmy Award nomination after *Too Soon for Jeff* was made into an ABC Afterschool Special, she is also the author of *I Won't Read and You Can't Make Me: Reaching Reluctant Teen Readers* (Heinemann, 2004). This is a practical guide for classroom teachers working with the "I hate to read" crowd. Marilyn Reynolds lives with her husband, Mike, in Gold River, California, and is the mother of three children who, thankfully, are way beyond their teen years. She enjoys her four grandchildren, traveling to new places, reading, and meeting with her readers at high schools and middle schools across the nation.

If you'd like to read more books by Marilyn Reynolds, here are some suggestions:

▶ *Detour for Emmy* (Buena Park, CA: Morning Glory Press, 1993), 256 pp.

Emmy's mother drinks too much; her brother is in trouble with the law; and her father is not on the scene. In spite of these difficulties, fifteen-year-old Emmy is a top-notch student until it's her turn for trouble. She's pregnant and her boyfriend denies that the baby is his.

▶ *Love Rules* (Buena Park, CA: Morning Glory Press, 2001), 269 pp.

At the beginning of their senior year in high school, Kit tells her best friend, Lynn, that she's a lesbian, she's tired of being in the closet, and she wants to live openly and honestly. Lynn's challenge, besides being attracted to someone of a different race, is to accept the "real" Kit and to understand Kit's struggles.

▶ *Telling* (Buena Park, CA: Morning Glory Press, 1996, c. 1989), 160 pp.

What should a twelve-year-old girl do after being accosted and fondled by the father of the children for whom she babysits? Feeling dirty and confused, Cassie is afraid to tell her parents and involves an older cousin in the mess.

To learn more about Marilyn Reynolds and her books, visit this website:
www.marilynreynolds.com

ABOUT JOHN H. RITTER

John H. Ritter is of German-Irish and Blackfoot Indian descent. He attributes his love for baseball and writing to his father and brothers, and he has passed on his passion for baseball to his daughter. In many of his interviews, he is quoted as saying that baseball is a great metaphor for life, so he uses the sport as a backdrop in his stories. He grew up in the rural hills of eastern San Diego County along the Mexican border and currently resides in both San Diego and on the island of Kauai with his wife, Cheryl. He is a full-time writer and speaks regularly at conferences held by such groups as the National Council of Teachers of English (NCTE), the International Reading Association (IRA), and the Assembly on Literature for Adolescents (ALAN).

If you'd like to read more books by John H. Ritter, here are some suggestions:

The Boy Who Saved Baseball (New York: Philomel Books, 2003), 224 pp.

One game decides whether or not the Dillontown baseball field will remain or become the site of a new development. Things look bleak for the diamond until a mysterious boy named Cruz de la Cruz rides into town, claiming to know the secret of hitting. (Note: Doubters of the legendary Cruz de la Cruz can visit the Cruz family's website at www.cruz-on.com.)

Choosing Up Sides (New York: Philomel Books, 1998), 176 pp.

Luke Bledsoe's father is a preacher who believes his son's left-handedness is the work of the devil. Imagine the difficulty when Luke, a talented southpaw, wants to join a baseball team.

Under the Baseball Moon (New York: Philomel Books, 2006), 224 pp.

Andy, who has aspirations of making it big in the music industry, meets Glory, a fast-pitch softball player who has big aspirations of her own, and together, these two crazy dreamers get tangled up in a mysterious plot on their way to fame and fortune.

To learn more about John H. Ritter and his books, visit this website:
www.johnhritter.com

ABOUT NEAL SHUSTERMAN

At the age of twenty-two, Neal Shusterman was the youngest syndicated columnist in the United States. Since then he has been successful as an author, screenwriter, television writer, film director, music writer, and playwright. He's also developed several "How to Host a Mystery" games—two for teenagers and five for adults. He's written for two well-known series, Goosebumps and Animorphs, and two of his novels—*Downsiders* and *The Dark Side of Nowhere*—are being considered for film. Neal enjoys writing for young adults because he hopes his books can help teenagers decide who they will be—as well as clarify their values and beliefs—by having strong characters to discuss.

If you'd like to read more books by Neal Shusterman, here are some suggestions:

▶ *Downsiders* (New York: Simon & Schuster, 1999), 244 pp.

Talon, a Downsider, falls in love with Lindsay, a Topsider. Readers will recognize the theme, similar to that of Hinton's *The Outsiders*, where social class separates and hurts people.

▶ *Everlost* (New York: Simon & Schuster, 2006), 317 pp.

Nick and Allie aren't quite dead, but they're not exactly alive either. After a car accident they find themselves in a magical and mysterious limbo between life and death called "Everlost." They must make an epic journey through a ghostly world to learn the true nature of reality, and to face their destiny.

▶ *The Schwa Was Here* (New York: Dutton, 2004), 276 pp.

Calvin Schwa is invisible, or at least that's what he and his classmates believe because "The Schwa" is never noticed—even when he's right there. From unraveling pranks to solving the mystery of "The

Schwa's" mother's disappearance, only one person has the power to tell everything he knows before "The Schwa Effect" takes over.

To learn more about Neal Shusterman and his books, visit this website:
www.storyman.com

ABOUT JERRY SPINELLI

Jerry Spinelli gets his ideas from his memories, the kids around him, and common occurrences in everyday life. He knew he wanted to be a writer after writing a poem about his high school football team's big victory that was published in a small newspaper. Jerry currently lives in Pennsylvania with his wife, Eileen, who is also a writer, and their six children. He and his family enjoy a good laugh whenever they can.

If you'd like to read more books by Jerry Spinelli, here are some suggestions:

The Library Card (New York: Scholastic, 1998, c. 1997), 148 pp.

Four teenagers share a story on how finding a library card altered each of their lives for the better.

Loser (New York: Joanna Cotler Books, 2002), 224 pp.

Donald Zinkoff is continually harassed, laughed at, and treated like a loser. Donald, however, proves that he is anything but that.

Stargirl (New York: Alfred A. Knopf, 2000), 192 pp.

After fifteen years of home schooling, Stargirl Caraway gets the opportunity to attend Micah High School. For Stargirl, trying to submit to the demands of peer pressure ends in disaster.

To learn more about Jerry Spinelli and his books, visit this website:
www.jerryspinelli.com

ABOUT SHELLEY STOEHR

In addition to receiving a Delacorte Press Honor Award for her first novel, which was published before she graduated from college, Shelley Stoehr spent time as a dancer, choreographer, and massage therapist. Now she prides herself on being a wife, mother, and writer. Shelley's trademark in her novels is reality, and she believes that young adult books are an effective way of communicating with teenagers. Using honesty when presenting the issues of sex and drugs is more beneficial to young adults, in her opinion, than trying to pretend they do not exist. It's not a preachy adult telling them, it's a character experiencing a situation relevant to their lives and being able to cope with it successfully. Her newest book, *Girl Broken*, deals with the issues of violence against teens, crystal meth addiction, and the trials of getting clean.

If you'd like to read more books by Shelley Stoehr, here are some suggestions:

▶ *Crosses* (Lincoln, NE: Writers Club Press, 2003, c. 1991), 161 pp.

Two best friends cut themselves purposely to relieve their emotional pain. One realizes that she needs help, but is it too late for her friend?

▶ *Tomorrow Wendy: A Love Story* (New York: Delacorte Press, 1998), 166 pp.

Cary and Danny are lovers, but secretly Cary really loves Danny's twin sister, Wendy. Raven, a lesbian who is new to their school, tries to help Cary with her feelings but things get all mixed up.

▶ *Weird on the Outside* (Lincoln, NE: Writers Club Press, 2003, c. 1995), 228 pp.

In this tragic story, a teenage girl runs away to New York City to escape from her divorced parents and begins working as a topless dancer to earn money.

To learn more about Shelley Stoehr and her books, visit this website:
http://shelleystoehr.com

ABOUT ANN TURNER

Ann Turner lives, breathes, and thinks books. They are as natural to her as breathing is to us. She attributes her love of reading to her father, who regularly used to bring home armloads of books so she could have at least a book a day. It is her mother, however, who encouraged her to write her first story at eight years of age—a story that she still has and shows to kids when she visits schools. Ann Turner currently lives in Massachusetts with her husband, two kids, and a big white poodle named Candy.

If you'd like to read more books by Ann Turner, here are some suggestions:

Hard Hit (New York: Scholastic, 2006), 128 pp.
   Fourteen-year-old Mark has a dad who's dying of cancer. Through poetry, Turner shares the progress of their time together, the inevitable ending, and how Mark copes with his loss, with the help of friends, faith, family, and baseball.

Learning to Swim (New York: Scholastic, 2000), 155 pp.
   Ann Turner's award-winning memoir uses poetry in a moving and powerful way to show how "telling" is the first and most important step in recovering from childhood sexual abuse.

A Lion's Hunger (Tarrytown, NY: Marshall Cavendish, 1998), 48 pp.

This short, award-winning book of poems follows one year in a girl's life as she experiences her first love. Turner eloquently reveals the reality of "firsts" from beginning to end—and all of the feelings in between—of a new relationship.

To learn more about Ann Turner and her books, visit this website:
www.annturnerbooks.com

ABOUT ELLEN WITTLINGER

Before becoming an award-winning novelist, Ellen Wittlinger worked as a librarian of children's books. Through her work, she learned of many talented young adult authors. This led her to want to write for this audience, which she finds enthralling. Ellen Wittlinger currently lives in a tiny town in Massachusetts with her husband, David. Ellen loves traveling, animals, and photography and recently enjoyed visiting her daughter in South Africa.

If you'd like to read more books by Ellen Wittlinger, here are some suggestions:

Hard Love (New York: Aladdin, 2002, c. 2000), 240 pp.

Marisol learns that John lost the emotional love and support from both of his parents after their divorce, causing him to shut down. When John starts having romantic feelings for her, Marisol must make it clear to him that she's not available.

Heart on My Sleeve (New York: Simon & Schuster, 2004), 224 pp.

Does Chloe love Julian or Eli, and just who does her older sister Genevieve love? Timing is everything in this story about discovering one's true self.

Sandpiper (New York: Simon & Schuster, 2005), 240 pp.

Sandy is a fifteen-year-old girl with a bad reputation for doing things with boys that she shouldn't. She befriends "Walker" and the two help each other in ways that surprise each other.

To learn more about Ellen Wittlinger and her books, visit this website:
www.ellenwittlinger.com

EDITOR'S NOTE

The idea for this book came while attending the 1999 Assembly on Literature for Adolescents (ALAN) in Denver, Colorado. As president of ALAN that year, I had the privilege of planning the workshop and its theme, "Saving Our Students' Lives through Literature and Laughter." Authors who wrote realistic fiction that addresses tough issues for teens shared their writing, their wisdom, their good intentions, and their laughter with us. I asked each of the authors if they had letters from teenagers that they couldn't throw away because "it was a piece of a child's soul and a person can't throw away a soul." My request resonated with many, so *Letters of Hope* was born.

Each author was asked to send me five to ten letters (though many exceeded that number), and I wrote a composite letter that protected the identities of each and every writer while attempting to capture the voice of a single child. Let it be known that the overriding themes contained in these letters were two very powerful ones: "Your book saved my life," and "I didn't know that anyone else existed who knew me!" Authors were then asked to write a "letter of hope" to the child so that their wisdom and writing talent could reach kids who are hurting.

I'm best known in the field of young adult literature for my work with teenagers who are both illiterate and in pain. Statistically, about 25 percent of our nation's youth have inordinate emotional issues (see *Adolescents At Risk: A Guide to Fiction and Nonfiction for Young Adults, Parents, and Professionals* and the six-volume series "Using Literature to Help Troubled Teenagers Cope," all from Greenwood Press). Many people resort to quick fixes or unhealthy escapes—alcohol and drugs, gangs and violence, cutting, eating disorders, rampant sex, even suicide—to get away from their pain.

We need to give teenagers better options—production of art (music, dance, theater) and crafts, athletics, a belief in a Higher Power, acts of service to humans and/or animals, and *literacy*. I am proud to say that books saved my life! In reading these children's letters, over and over again, the same themes emerged: "You saved my life!" "I'm not alone." "You wrote about me." "Thank you!"

So thank you for picking up this book. Reading (and writing) are healthy escapes until a person is able to or old enough to address her or his pain. For those who like what particular authors have to say, please use the information about the authors and their books, as well as their website addresses, to learn more. Remember, there's hope in a book!!!

Be well and create peace,
Joan F. Kaywell